One Foot in Front
of the Other

The Author

Teena Gates is 98FM Head of News and has spent two decades as a working journalist in Dublin. Two years after her dramatic weight loss, Teena has a passion for rock-climbing and horse riding. She cycles 15k to work, goes to the gym at least twice a week, swims in the Irish Sea most weekends, and is currently learning to sea kayak. This is her first book.

One Foot in Front of the Other

Teena Gates

Gill & Macmillan

Gill & Macmillan
Hume Avenue, Park West, Dublin 12
with associated companies throughout the world
www.gillmacmillan.ie

© Teena Gates 2012
978 07171 5369 5

Typography design by Make Communication
Print origination by Síofra Murphy
Printed by ScandBook AB, Sweden

This book is typeset in Minion 14/17 pt.

The paper used in this book comes from the wood pulp of
managed forests. For every tree felled, at least one tree is planted,
thereby renewing natural resources.

A CIP catalogue record for this book is available from the
British Library.

5 4 3 2 1

Contents

Foreword

Renowned Irish adventurer, author, film-maker and motivational leader Pat Falvey is the first person in the world to climb the seven highest mountains on the seven continents twice—including Mount Everest. He has walked to the South Pole in honour of the famous Irish Antarctic explorer Ernest Shackleton, and is currently attempting to walk to the North Pole. In 2010, he met Teena Gates when she had already set out on her mission to lose 12 stone and had ambitions to trek to Base Camp Mount Everest.

I first met Teena as she arrived down to the Mountain Lodge here in Killarney, at 16 stone, and with a desire to trek to Everest Base Camp. She had already lost a staggering 7 stone. I was intrigued by her bouncy attitude to life as she spoke on the phone of the journey she'd already begun. She was full of exuberance, with a gung-ho attitude, ready to take on what she believed would be the biggest challenge of her life. Listening to her enthusiasm, I gladly invited her down to the Lodge.

On the morning of her arrival we had a group of people ready to climb Carrauntoohil, which Teena had said would, at this point, be her Everest. To my horror, four very healthy and energetic climbers arrived for the day ahead; they were what I would consider to be athletic individuals. As we were having tea, a voice rang out from the utility room and a delighted Teena bounced into the group, with purple leggings and leotard, her belly rolling stubbornly between the two. Everyone stared, and I found myself thinking, 'Oh feck, what are we going out with today?' I strode across the ensuing silence to give Teena a warm hug and welcome her to the Mountain Lodge. Looking at the table around me, the group was clearly in dismay and I could see they were thinking, 'We'll not make the summit today.' Taking into consideration that I may have misjudged the team, I emphasised at the briefing that this was a group team effort. Consciously thinking of Teena, I repeated the point that we would be moving to the speed of the slowest person. Everyone agreed to this and we headed off.

To my own astonishment, as the day progressed and we moved speedily up on what indeed turned out to be most of the group's own private Everest—Carrauntoohil, Teena astounded everyone. They were blown away by her eagerness, tenacity and ability to literally dance like a butterfly over the scrambling route that I'd chosen for the day. Even more to my surprise, the athletic types of the team were under severe pressure. On arriving to the summit, it felt like

I had travelled back to my second time on the hill, when I first said I would climb Mount Everest; there, Teena, with a tear in her eye and emotion in her voice, told me she felt like she was 'on top of the world'.

The fat girl on the mountain could have been written off. But I was bowled over, and indeed jubilant, to see the power of the mind over the body. I watched a story being etched on a mountain in front of my own eyes, of how the will to achieve can make the impossible possible. I looked at her fervour, flair, passion and conviction, and knew that once again I was looking at someone who had a goal and was going to achieve it through the power of the mind, commitment, desire, and the hunger to succeed. I accepted that I had a new team member and thus the journey began. Read on . . .

Pat Falvey
Mountain Lodge, Killarney
November 2011

How I Found Hope

I was jubilant and I found myself searching for a way to say thanks to the universe for changing my life. I had shed several stone to successfully undergo vital gall bladder surgery, my chronic back pain had disappeared and my body had changed from 23 stone to a healthier 16 stone. As I looked for a way to express my joy, a lady from The Hope Foundation charity was also searching—for volunteers to participate in a celebrity charity climb to Base Camp on Mount Everest, the highest mountain in the world. When we collided on Facebook I felt as if fate had knocked on my door, and climbing my own personal Everest took on a whole new meaning.

The Hope Foundation works to free children and poor families from lives of pain, abuse, poverty and darkness. I didn't realise it at the time, but on this occasion, it also gave me hope. As a journalist I have always had plenty of access to the darker shades of our world: the misery, poverty and pain that surround us. I wrote about it but also distanced myself from it, perhaps for fear of being overwhelmed. While happy to throw loose coins in a bucket or buy a ticket for a charity ball, I had never attempted to actively participate in fundraising or engage in charitable works myself. I always felt the problems were too vast and I could make no difference.

When I met The Hope Foundation's Rosaleen Thomas to discuss my joining her Hope/Everest team, she explained that HOPE stands for 'Help One Person Everyday'. That conversation changed my life, as I wondered how many people I could have helped if I had executed that mission every day of my 46 years. Today I know that I have made a difference and I know that I can continue to make a difference. A donation from sales of this book will go towards The Hope Foundation, which is a registered charity working with the street and slum children of Kolkata (formerly Calcutta), India. Photographer Hugh Chaloner, who was part of our HOPE/Everest team, is also donating his professional fee for photographs of his which are used here to document my journey.

Background

Set up in 1999 to raise funds for one girls' home, The Hope Foundation is a registered Irish charity with branch offices in India, the UK, Germany and the USA. It now works with 14 Indian partner organisations to rescue thousands of children from the streets and slums of Kolkata. To date, through education alone, HOPE has reached out to almost 30,000 children, and its primary healthcare programme, in partnership with Irish Aid, has reached hundreds of thousands of the poorest children and vulnerable families. Living on the streets, children are exposed to horrendous physical, emotional, economic and sexual abuses. Those who survive are left to fend for themselves, with no promise of a safe future. They are forced to work from as young as five years of age to earn money for food and so cannot go to school. HOPE works to free them from child labour. HOPE funds and operates over 60 projects, reaching out to those most forgotten, and offering protection, healthcare, nutrition, education, rehabilitation, love and a family for life.

Director's Message

'For the poorest people in our global community, the recession has meant a stark reduction in even the barest essentials for living. This means going from a life of bare subsistence to one of uncertainty, insecurity, more suffering and quite often, premature death. There are no safety nets, such as social welfare, for the families we work with. Their survival is determined by your generosity and kindness in reaching out and responding in whatever way you can. I ask you to remember the street and slum children and to support our work.'

Maureen Forrest
Honorary Director (voluntary)
The Hope Foundation
Registered Charity No. 13237

Chapter 1
Mermaid on Ice

Hanging from the headwall, my weight bearing down on my crampons, the ferocious metal spikes strapped to my ice boots and dug into the ice, my leg muscles screaming and my breath laboured, I wonder again how I could find myself here. A year ago I weighed in at 23 stone. Just 5 ft high and as wide as I was long, I couldn't imagine walking to the shop; and yet I've made it this far—to the highest mountain in the world. I've made it to Base Camp Mount Everest and even further. Here today and still travelling in the Himalayas, I'm within grasping distance of the summit of Island Peak, 20,305 ft high, and close to the top of the world. I've spent a year getting here, and two weeks in Nepal getting to this point, tackling sickness and altitude every step of the way. Now I've reached the final challenge. Can I do it? I've no strength left and I'm only two-thirds of the way up this impossible expanse of frozen snow. Even if I make it up here, there's still a long, dizzying and dangerous walk along a narrow ridge, before finally reaching the tiny 6 ft circumference of the summit. I have absolutely no idea how I can make it up this final stretch. My ice axe in my left hand digs into the ice, my jumar ascender, which helps me to push upwards, clamps my harness to a fixed rope. For a moment I rest, look up to the top of the frozen wall, close my eyes briefly, and think about how the journey began. My mind transports me from this frozen rock to the warmth of the Med and how my battle to get here started as I swam in the sea off the South of France, over a year ago . . .

Back then the sun felt hot on my face as the waves carried me away from the shore in a wash of colour and warmth. Striking out with my left arm, I watched my fingers edge downwards to cut through the water in front, laughing at the freedom of movement, of being supported by the silken touch of a fragrant sea. Rolling onto my back, I looked up at the cliffs, searching out my favourite villas, amazed at the way they clung to the edge of the rocks, making up stories about their owners and wishing I was one of them. Swimming here in the water, I did imagine for a while that I belonged with the beautiful people; with my bulk hidden beneath the waves and just my arms and my face on view. At a tiny 5 ft in height and weighing more than twice the normal weight for my size, I was out of place on the shore—the image of a beached whale came to mind. But in the water I could move freely and I felt beautiful again; whale turned mermaid for as long as I played in the tide, as long as my feet didn't touch the ground, tales of Oisín* in my mind.

Rolling back, I swam out further from the shore and looked towards the fishing boats moored out at sea, beyond them the yachts and beyond them the massive cruise ships that came in early in the morning and left at night, flooding the little French fishing village with flocks of American tourists bound for Nice and Monaco. They passed through quickly, rarely lingering in the village, and their floating palaces were gone again by sunset, leaving the waterfront to those who knew her best. Villefranche-sur-Mer, the little French fishing village by the sea, nestled between the party city of Nice and the glamour of Monaco, beautiful, ancient and unspoiled by its glamorous neighbours. It's a place I discovered years ago and have returned to many times, and it is here I came to get well.

Reaching out for the shore, I swam slowly, amazed again at the warmth of the sea, the brightness of the

---

*Oisín: *Oisín is a legendary Irish adventurer swept away by the love of a fairy woman to Tír na nÓg, the 'land of eternal youth'. After three years, Oisín returns to Ireland but finds 300 years have passed. He's warned not to dismount from his magic horse or time will catch up with him as his feet touch the ground. Our hero falls from his mount while helping some men to move a stone from the road and the prophecy is realised. Oisín withers and dies and the magic horse returns to Tír na nÓg.*

day, and the crystal clarity of the water as it splashed from my arms, glistening and sparkling in the sun. I felt good and I felt strong. The surf broke as I neared the shore, and I landed on my knees on the beach. I'd been in the water a long time, and my legs shook as I tried to stand up. I took a minute to balance my weight on one foot and then the other and, finally standing, I inched forward towards the rocks, reached for my walking stick and limped painfully up the beach to my towel and picnic lunch. A mermaid doesn't cope too well on two feet.

I'd left Dublin on a budget flight and come to France on a mission. I was 23 stone, with chronic back pain. I couldn't jog or run, could hardly walk, but I needed an operation and I somehow had to lose 4 stone in a hurry. So here I began, joking to my friends that I was on the 'red wine and olive diet', and in a way I was. I booked in to the Welcome Hotel for two weeks on my own, determined to make a start. Swimming was the only exercise I felt I could tackle at the moment. My back still hurt while I swam but at least it didn't go into spasm like it did when I tried to walk. For food, there seemed no hardship in eating fish fresh from the sea in one of a dozen little restaurants perched out along the waterfront, feeding the bread basket to the fishes instead of myself, while I ate olives instead. The fish hovered in the water beside the tables, hungrily waiting for my donations, and the waiter insisted there was a shark there. I think he must have had Irish blood because he was great at spinning yarns. I was convinced I could almost see a flash of dorsal fins before I headed back to the hotel. The warmth here was wonderful, and coming from a place of pain and fear it was welcome and comforting.

When people heard about my back pain, they saw my size and shape first and presumed I was just lazy and suffering the well-earned effects of gluttony and lack of exercise. That wasn't the case but it was too exhausting to keep explaining. The problem started with a fall from a horse nearly a decade ago. I was fit and active at the time but I totally took my health for granted. I dived, I rode horses and I swam around 40 lengths most days. I did it all for fun and never thought of myself as an athlete or someone who was physically strong. When I hurt my back, I stopped all the activity but never thought to change the way I ate. I don't have a sweet tooth, then or now, but I ate lots of protein and fats, red meat and dairy, and basically filled my body with fuel it no longer needed. There wasn't really anything wrong with the food that I was eating but I was simply eating too much. I didn't realise my portion sizes were too large for someone who wasn't exercising regularly. I was blissfully ignorant of the damage I was causing myself, until I woke up one morning and realised for the first time that I was seriously overweight. I went out and bought larger clothes and a fried chicken snack box to console myself, and a cycle began.

I'd be lying if I didn't confess to sometimes using the back pain as an excuse for not exercising. But it's too simple to blame one totally on the other and it's not what happened. The pain came first, long before the weight. Can you imagine waking up and having to roll from your bed to the floor to ease out the kinks before you can even begin to get moving? You suffer all day, do a full day's work, then roll back home and crawl into bed at night, digging your thumbs into the muscle beside your spine to try and ease it out so that you can sleep. I did that every day for almost a decade and nobody knew why. I went to doctors, hospitals, physios, chiropractors, got x-rayed, needled and massaged and reliably informed there was 'nothing wrong with me'. My heart goes out to people with chronic pain. You can't display any cuts or bruises and people can't really see or understand your suffering no matter how well intentioned they may be. You get tired talking about your pain and feel you're boring people, so you suffer in silence, and man, you suffer. You get used to the pain but pain is so exhausting, so depressing, it sucks the life energy from your soul. At times I did wonder if I was going mad. Was I imagining it? Why couldn't the doctors find something wrong? Perhaps this was just the normal condition, everyone felt like this and I was just making a big deal of it. Was I losing my mind? Your back is your core, so when it hurts, everything hurts; sitting, standing, lying down—everything you do is affected. I never thought it would be my life forever, though; I never gave up hope that I'd wake up one morning and the pain would go away.

Weighing in as two people—23 stone—brought a whole new set of problems; things that people probably don't think about. Could I get a seat if I walked into a pub, because I wouldn't be able to stand for long? If I met friends for coffee, would I be able to sit on the chair, would I fit into it? If I did, would it hold my frame or would it break? It happened to me twice and on one occasion a group of people broke up laughing when I landed on my ass on the floor. I was good at breaking furniture. In the days of Celtic Tiger Ireland I spent €5,000 on a new couch—puff, it collapsed, twice. The company agreed to fix it, twice, but they were baffled and I had to ask a friend to let the repair man in, in case he saw me and refused to honour the guarantee under some exclusion for fat people!

Airports were a nightmare: walking to the departure gate with my weight dragging me down and my back locking in spasm and forcing me to fall to a knee, pretending to adjust a shoe strap or check something about my luggage. Finally I resorted to being brought to the gate by one of those little motorised trucks that the airport arranges for older people and those with physical disabilities. When I finally made it to the plane, would I fit in the seat? I work as a journalist, heading up a radio newsroom in

Dublin and frequently reporting stories about airlines considering charging extra fares for larger people; each time I knew the story could be written about me. Each time I approached a trip I suffered terrors that this time I wouldn't fit. I was already familiar with asking for the extension belts that I needed to make the safety belt fit, pinning a smile on my face and determined not to show any embarrassment as I asked for the add-on clips usually reserved for pregnant women. The first time I couldn't get the standard-sized belt to close was pure torture. I didn't even realise there were extension belts then; I had to confess to the steward that I couldn't fix the belt and had to go through the agony of the explanation, terrified that I'd be taken off the flight. Afterwards, knowledge made the process a little easier. Ironically, eating food in flight was out of the question, because I couldn't pull down the food tray. I could probably have balanced a plate on top of my belly, but it was all too mortifying, so much easier to just go without.

I wonder if all confident people are terrified along with their courage. I know I sometimes feel that way. Those who know me believe I'm confident, assertive, assured and totally happy with myself. Those who know me well know that I can often be a scared little mouse who quakes before walking into a room and baulks at talking to strangers. I always protest to people that I'm shy but most don't believe it. They're wrong. I'm just a really good actor using smoke and mirrors to draw a veil over who's in the house: the lion or the mouse. When there's no alternative, I put on my confidence like I put on a winter coat.

It may seem like a contradiction that someone like me ends up working in radio, but I often joke that my job basically consists of sitting on my own in a padded cell—as the soundproofed radio studio might sometimes be described! I manage a team of people and I love being responsible for hiring new young talent and setting them off on careers in such a wonderful medium that I love so well. When I'm broadcasting, I speak to a microphone and choose to presume that I'm speaking to one person, rather than thousands. Work is demanding, creative, absorbing, I love it, and it distracted me from the pain in my back. Being in radio, it is also less important than on TV to look a certain way. I still can't believe I gained weight up to the point of 23 stone without doing anything about it. I was in denial, and everyone around me was too polite to shake me out of it. In a way we were all complicit in a big secret. Teena wasn't well, but no one knew what to do about it—least of all Teena.

So why the change, why then? Why this new determination to lose 4 stone and why the South of France? It wasn't looking in the mirror that made a difference, it wasn't something someone said and it wasn't anything on TV or in a magazine. I didn't just wake up one morning with a burning ambition to shake off my second self and aim for a size 10. If I'm honest, my motivator was simple and possibly one of the strongest human drivers—fear. I ended up in hospital for three weeks, with terrible stomach pain and nausea. I was diagnosed with a diseased gall bladder and told that it had to be removed, which at my weight was a very dangerous and complicated procedure. The consultant gave me two stark choices: an 8-inch incision with a high-risk result, or keyhole surgery which he could only attempt if I lost at least 4 stone. I had never received a single stitch as a child, had never broken a bone, was never in hospital. The horror of what lay ahead totally terrified me. I certainly knew I favoured the prospect of keyhole surgery over the alternative and knew which route I was taking. But I saw the look of doubt in the consultant's eye when I told him I'd lose the fat. I knew he didn't believe I could do it, but I also knew with total certainty that I would. I was due holidays, and I booked them shortly afterwards, heading to familiar territory on the Riviera, to one of the prettiest places on the planet and my then spiritual home to kick-start my newest challenge.

Looking back I can see that my effort to get well started with a firm decision, not just an aspiration or realisation; my decision to get well happened when I got sick that summer. You could say I had hit rock bottom, and I definitely was looking death in the face. Along with the need for an operation the doctor also warned me that I had a fatty liver, my cholesterol was off the chart and I was borderline diabetic.

Maybe that was the first turning point—I didn't just 'hope' to lose weight any more, I had added determination to the mix and decided to do it.

The suntan, the exercise and two weeks of healthy eating in France had already made a difference to my spirit as I landed back in Dublin Airport. Two weeks away from my very busy schedule and the indulgence of just being with myself for a fortnight probably had a role to play too. Coming back, I felt great and I felt confident that what I had started in France I could continue at home. I had lost weight through my three weeks of illness in hospital and had lost more swimming and eating olives and fresh fish in France, so I had already made a start.

I had learned a great lesson in hospital. It had taken three weeks for the medic to get the poisons from my diseased gall bladder under control and shortly before I was released they arranged for me to speak to a nutritionist. I wasn't impressed. I'm a girl, I understand calories and fats and proteins, I can tell you how many calories are in a pot of yogurt; I reckoned I knew all there was to know about food. What could a nutritionist tell me that I didn't already know? The nutritionist arrived—and at first she didn't speak about food at all. 'Where do you work?' she asked. 'Do you hold meetings? How long do the meetings last? How long do you spend preparing for them?' I explained that depending on the meeting I could spend up to 20 minutes preparing at home before I arrived into work. Yes, I agreed on further questioning, I do have projects underway for next month and yes, I have a vague outline of what I might have planned for the end of the year.

She leaned forward towards me, catching my eyes with hers. 'What's in your fridge?' I was stumped, because I genuinely didn't have a clue. I could not tell her what was in my fridge or my cupboard. 'So,' she said, 'you'll prepare and plan for meetings at work that haven't even happened, but you can't take five minutes to plan your diet, when eating is the single most important function of your life.' When I suggested that was a bit of a stretch, she pressed on. 'Eating and drinking are more important than loving and being loved. You can't continue to look after a child or love another human, if you're not strong enough to survive.' Perhaps seeing a look of cynicism in my eye, she tried again: 'Looking after yourself isn't a selfish goal; it's just a normal function of living,' she said, adding, 'Even on a plane, the emergency drill advises parents to put the oxygen mask on themselves first, and then tend to their children.'

It was a powerful lesson and I 'got it'. Maybe it's a female thing, but I've always been brought up to consider everyone else first and myself last. This was my first lesson on the importance of being kind to me. Now I want to shout to everyone loud and clear:

'Be kind to yourself.' It's not a sign of weakness and it's not selfish; loving yourself is a tribute to your own humanity and the first step in being strong enough to look after others.

I was challenged and I was motivated but I still wasn't informed. I finally realised that I might believe I knew a lot about food but I didn't actually know very much about nutrition. I knew that I needed to find a way to lose weight in a sustained way, over a long period of time. I couldn't do it by starvation and I had to come up with a way of dieting that didn't bore me or torture me into submission! I looked around for help and found it in the shape of WeightWatchers. Lots of people will have different successful ways of losing weight, it's about finding what works for you, but you'll never succeed if you're doing it for someone else: you have to want to do it for you. I knew that before I walked into the first meeting.

I can remember that first meeting vividly ...

The parish hall is cold. Walking through the door I feel branded as a fat person, as if everyone on the street can see me walking up the path and guess why I am there. Hurrying inside to avoid the invisible audience, I find a queue and furtively glance around, deciding quickly that I'm the largest lady in the room. It's not exactly reassuring. Falling back on my fake confidence, I pin on my brightest smile, pay my fee and head towards the weighing room. More embarrassment as I step on the scales but no sense of judgment from the smiling class leader as I take my paperwork and move back outside to the main hall and the rest of the class. Listening, the lecture makes sense; no such thing as good foods and bad foods, just calories and fats, fuels in and fuels out. I stay back afterwards as is the tradition and am talked through the points system and how members track what they eat and how much they exercise. As I get up to go I comment 'I can do the diet, but I won't do the walking.' Considering how the next 12 months would follow on, the words have acquired a special significance for me.

My first and biggest WeightWatchers lesson was to do with portion size. Under my new regime I needed to calculate the amount of energy that food would give me based on its ingredients. The system gave me a set of values to work out how many ProPoints worth of food I could eat in a day, then track what I'm eating and count the points. For example, if I worked out a menu that included 6 ounces of steak, I then needed to measure out 6 ounces of steak to eat and if I went over the agreed measurement, something else would need to be trimmed back. It seemed very simple to me and perfectly fair. I did a really good supermarket shop and came home with a bunch of striploin steaks—delighted with myself. I would weigh them out, perhaps need to trim a bit off the edge, and put them away in the freezer all ready for cooking at a future date. I pulled out the weighing scales and got to work, quickly horrified when I realised that for a 'normal' portion, I practically had to cut the steaks in half. In the past I would have eaten two! Realisation quickly dawned that I simply had been eating good food, but in crazy amounts.

Under the new plan I found I was eating more frequently than ever before, and actually eating more food, but different types of food in different proportions. Salad for me used to be a garnish on the corner of a plate, but now, with fat-free dressings and a sprinkling of nuts or shavings of Parmesan cheese, it was making up 60 per cent of the food on the plate. I was eating more fish and trying out new foods. I discovered the wonderful tastes and aromas of herbs and spices. I began each day with cereal and fruit and yogurt, swapped full-fat milk to soya milk and stayed away from sugary colas. My WeightWatchers leader, Vera Baker, later told classes that she had a good idea I was on the right track when I spoke at the second meeting. I apparently said that I wasn't on a diet, but 'on a journey to discover new and amazing foods'. I think there's definitely a lesson there: Developing healthy eating habits doesn't have to be boring or painful. There is life after diet!

When I began to keep a food diary and track my food intake and frequency of meals, I quickly realised that I had a terrible routine. Working the early morning shift as a breakfast news presenter, I woke at 4 a.m., started work at 5 a.m. and worked until 4 p.m., when I ate my first meal of the day. It seems outrageous now, but for over a decade that was my routine and it wasn't the fault of the job; I completely did it to myself. I would never feel hungry getting up in the middle of the night and once I started on my daily routine of coffee and adrenaline I never felt hungry until I left work. By that time, I was too exhausted to cook something sensible and ended up picking up a take-out on the way home. I always attributed my tiredness to the early start and never realised that I had been starving my body and running myself into the ground for the whole day. It simply never occurred to me that I was injuring myself and since going on this journey of mine and talking to lots of other people, I've realised I'm not the only one to go down that path.

A couple of months into my new eating regime, I had a particularly rushed start to the day and started getting vicious cramps in my stomach. Holding my side, I got increasingly concerned, and mentioned to my staff that I might have to leave. They looked at me oddly as, a few minutes later, I suddenly burst out laughing. I had just heard my stomach rumble and realised in an instant that I had missed breakfast and was feeling hunger pangs for the first time in a decade. My body finally trusted me enough to send messages again. For so long I had starved and gorged my own senses into submission and here was recovery breakthrough number one. I could listen to my own body and it would tell me when I was hungry and when I was thirsty; I could now follow my body's logic instead of the clock on the wall. I instantly recognised the importance of those hunger pangs the moment I felt them. I also ate breakfast!

Learning to eat healthily in my own home was a challenge and as soon as I felt I had some kind of system going at home, I then needed to take my new skills out on the town. It was a challenge in itself to look at a restaurant menu and calculate a low-fat option. WeightWatchers is based on learning how to live normally while losing weight and maintaining weight loss, so the art of pointing and tracking while eating out was simply another life skill that I needed to get my head around. It took a while, and boy, did I get it wrong. My first attempt was a late breakfast in the city with a gal pal. I decided against my normal favourite full Irish breakfast with puddings and bacon and sausages and soda farls. With huge effort I turned away and surveyed the menu instead for healthy alternatives. My friend Kerry's eyes glazed over and her stomach groaned as I painfully debated the options. Eggs Béarnaise with spinach sounded healthy; spinach does, doesn't it? Well as you probably already know or can guess, it certainly wasn't low-fat. I am no master chef and I had no idea that Béarnaise sauce is made almost entirely from butter. My painstakingly chosen breakfast probably had the combined calorie intake of a full Irish and then some! That week I gained a pound. I'm sure it wasn't just the Béarnaise, but it's an example of how easy it is to get it wrong.

There were lots of blips like that, but I kept learning. The day I sent a dish back politely because they had included sauce on the salmon when I asked for it nude, I realised that making choices in a restaurant is simply a case of being clear about what you want and politely insisting that you get what you asked for. In fact, when I got over the embarrassment of the first few times, I discovered that chefs and waiters were generally delighted to help when I asked for low-fat options. They are generally thrilled that customers will engage with them on menus and are usually really helpful and interested in return. If they aren't, I simply don't give them my business in the future. It's about losing the embarrassment and realising that you're a customer with needs which might be slightly different from the norm, but a customer nonetheless and deserving of good service.

My second trip back to WeightWatchers wasn't a huge success—I'd only lost a pound and I had expected to have lost more, but I told myself it was a start. I also found I was interested in some of the other ladies' stories, and I found myself sharing my disastrous breakfast experience. There were howls of laughter but it was sympathetic, shared hilarity and it didn't sting. I felt part of a group, a gang, less isolated. All of a sudden I didn't feel I was totally alone, that I was odd or that my experience was totally unique. Even now, I look at those ladies with such respect and affection. It takes guts to walk into a meeting and share your fear and shame with strangers and they welcomed me into their hearts. I honestly don't know if I could have lost weight on my own. Maybe I could have, but I'm glad I didn't have to. Ladies of Dublin 15, you are my friends and my inspiration.

Every week as I listened to the tips about what worked and what didn't, the one area where I didn't have experiences to share was when it came to talking about exercising and walking. Finally I started to look around for something I could do that wouldn't hurt my back. I knew I could get away with swimming— it hurt, but I could do it. I paid another visit back to the doctor, asking for straight answers. Did he think it would make it any worse if I put pressure on it? 'No.' The answer was clear enough and it was enough for me to push forward to a new stage. If my back couldn't get any worse, perhaps it could get a little better, and if it hurt so what the heck? Pain was one thing I understood. So I started swimming. It hurt, but it also felt good. For the first time in years, I felt I was taking back control and it wasn't just my weight I was battling; I was battling against the way my back had held me captive for so many years. I started remembering all the wonderful sports and fun that used to be part of my day and wondered how I had managed to let all that slip away. Well, I was finally changing that. As I began to swim regularly, I got thinking again and wondered about yoga. I'd always had an interest in yoga but had never tried it. I had heard it was gentle and kind to the body, so I thought it wouldn't harm to have a go at least and see if my back would let me get away with it. I hadn't a clue what I was looking for, so I signed up for the first local class that I could find and I paid in advance before I got a chance to change my mind.

I felt nervous as I parked in the car park outside the local gym. I wasn't really sure what to wear. I expected I'd have to walk through a gauntlet of svelte, beautiful, winsome wonders in skinny leggings and tight tops. People who exercise on TV wear leotards and leggings and look toned and fit and I knew I didn't look the part. I couldn't fit into a leotard and even if one existed in my size, I'd probably be arrested for wearing it! I dragged myself out of the car, walked towards the opening arch to the gym and with a certain amount of trepidation pushed open the door. Bright lights and fit, healthy people in various stages of physical exertion instantly surrounded me; there were complicated-looking exercise machines lined up the whole way to reception. It was worse than I'd imagined it would be. I was terrified. I didn't belong and wasn't sure where to look. I pinned on my 'confidence' face and asked the pretty girl on reception where the yoga classes were. In fairness she smiled and there was no hint of surprise or disdain in her eye as she looked at me and pointed out where I needed to go. I turned towards the stairs and started plodding up towards the studio on the first floor in my baggy tracks and men's xxxl sweater, one step at a time and using the banister to pull myself along.

There were no winsome wonders; skinny and svelte yes, fit looking yes, a couple of average-looking lasses, a couple of wobbly wonders—and me. I pulled up a mat and joined in. Jesus, the pain in my wrists: 23 stone hanging upside down balancing on your hands and feet is a pretty painful place to be and looking back it can't have been a pretty sight either. But no one cared; we were all too focused on getting our bodies into the shapes the leader was showing us. I didn't care how the others looked and pretty soon I realised that they didn't care about me. I found the class tough, almost impossible to keep up with, and some sections I just couldn't manage. But surprisingly there were a couple of moves that I could really pull off, even on that first night and even with the state my body was in. I was astounded: I still had some flexibility and my body was eager to respond where and when it could. I felt encouraged and as I cooled down and listened to the leader at the end of the class asking us to thank our bodies, I found I was happy with myself. As I left, I considered whether I'd return and decided that if I could get through the first class, there was no reason why I couldn't get through a second. Later I learned that Ashtanga yoga was probably one of the most difficult disciplines I could have chosen as an introduction. But I persisted at the time and ended up loving it. Yoga went on to be a part of my life, and continues to be a gentle, healing, wonderful influence.

A couple of weeks of walking through the gym to yoga classes left me a little less intimidated by the disciples of fitness and their shiny machines. Ironically, I already owned a membership for this gym. I jokingly called it a 'pay as you go' scheme, where you sign up some January with a direct debit, get the free gym bag—and then go away. I'd been paying for years for a gym that I never used and to my surprise I later learned that lots of people do that. Was I convincing myself that someday I'd use it or was it an extension of the 'my diet starts tomorrow' club? I truly don't know. I was obviously kidding myself and in some form of denial. But now, swimming regularly and learning yoga, I started thinking again. Maybe instead of just cancelling the gym membership, I should actually have a go at making use of it. What did I have to lose? As part of the gym membership you get a consultation with one of the gym's fitness instructors and I thought that asking them for help and advice was a good place to start.

To put all this new-found activity in context: I was still walking with a stick. I didn't bring the cane into work because I felt it exposed my weakness. I told friends later that it felt easier to be considered lazy than disabled and I wasn't sure then or now why that was the case. One of my colleagues thought it was a control issue, that perhaps I didn't want to lose face— maybe that was the case, I'm not sure. But I'd make it into work and park outside on the street, get into the lift, arrive at my desk and stay there all day. My car kept getting clamped because I couldn't make it down to put money in the meter. It was a long-standing joke in the office that I was the most clamped motorist in Dublin. I casually threw my eyes to heaven, sighed deeply and agreed, talking of the injustice of the clampers and waving off my train of bad luck with explanations that I 'got so involved' in writing news stories that I'd forget to go down and feed the meter. I'm sure people thought I was being strange, but I convinced myself that I got away with it. The truth of the matter was that making it down four flights of stairs and out to the meter was just too tough—even standing in the lift was agony, with my 23 stone pushing down on my size 4 feet, but there was no way I could bring myself to tell my colleagues that I was that bad. I'm still asking myself why I was so embarrassed to admit I was in pain when everyone could clearly see I was obese. It must have been denial kicking in again.

I wouldn't eat at all during the day and I wouldn't go down to the kitchen to make coffee because it was on the third floor and it was just too much hassle to make it down there, even with the lift. There was a long corridor to navigate, lined with desks on either side, and that rite of passage was something I avoided as much as possible. I hated to be seen limping and basically stayed trapped at my desk until my day's work was done. It was nobody's fault except my own. No one knew and I went to great lengths to ensure they didn't find out. There was always help there if I needed it, but I just didn't ask for it. I worked the morning breakfast news shift and my lifestyle was terrible when it came to diet and exercise. I would wake up at 4 a.m., would dash off to work, and wouldn't really eat anything until I got home in the afternoon, when I would open the fridge and graze in front of the telly before going to bed. It's not the best way to keep your metabolism in good shape. Since then, I've come across similar stories from people suffering from overweight. Time and time again I hear about people not bothering or forgetting to eat in the morning, going without food for hours, and then wondering how they could possibly be facing a weight problem.

I can remember making this conscious effort to change my diet, but I can't really remember sitting down and planning an exercise regime—other than deciding not to do any! However, one day, on my way into one of my yoga classes at the gym, I found myself halting at reception and making an appointment to see an instructor. I was introduced to a chap called David Dunne. I explained honestly about my sickness, my lack of fitness and my back pain and basically said, 'I can't walk, I can't run, I can't do very much at all, but I've got to lose weight for an operation and I want a programme to make that happen.' I thought David looked very young and probably wouldn't understand. I hadn't put much thought into this and as I heard myself speaking, I could hear the extent of the challenge I was throwing him. I thought it sounded silly and impossible, but David didn't hesitate: 'No problem, let's do this,' he said, and we were off.

The first time I walked on a treadmill, I walked for one minute—just one minute. I can't stress that enough for anyone who's thinking about getting active after a long break. I literally could not walk for longer than one minute on the treadmill. I was hanging on to the arms of the machine, dragging myself along and putting one foot in front of the other, while I wheezed and groaned and thought I was going to die. I was sweating, my heart was pounding, and my back muscles kept seizing up. But the next time, I walked for two minutes, and after that I got to go for five. That was my routine for a time, five minutes on the treadmill and then on to weights. I loved weights. David had knowledge that helped me work my body and build up strength regardless of my weaknesses. He never allowed me to use the pain in my back or the way my back would seize up as an excuse for not exercising. He explained about 'training smart' and I learned that you can always find a way to be active. Even if you've been injured, you can still train around it. It was another one of those life lessons: life doesn't have to stop if you're hurting, you just find another way to live.

The gym provides you with a programme and their instructors don't have to check on you again for several weeks or until you approach them for a new assessment. He didn't have to be, but David was always around to check my progress, move the programme forward and offer an encouraging word. He was absolutely marvellous and from the beginning I felt he was part of 'Team Teena'.

I was still turning up for my weekly WeightWatchers meetings, and with my new exercise regime and my new healthy eating regime, the pounds were really coming off. I was up and at it, on course and on programme, and then I started thinking about the reason why I had started my new lifestyle.

The operation that I needed weighed heavy on my mind. I was scared and I felt I needed more information. I have always responded to a new challenge or fear by learning as much as I can about the threat. So I googled everything I could find about gall bladders, operations and keyhole surgery; NOT such a good idea if you don't want to be terrified.

Every single permutation and complication was written out somewhere online for me to find and I found them all. End result? Well, of course I terrified myself even more.

I started thinking about the public and my job, and how I should manage the news of my operation. Working in the media, I knew that I needed to decide up front whether I wanted the operation to be private or whether I'd be comfortable talking about it in public. For reasons equally selfish and generous, I decided to talk about it. I thought that if there were other people out there terrified like me about an operation, it might be helpful to them to hear about my experiences . . . but I also hoped I'd hear from other people who'd been through the process, to reassure me! So I went on social media like Facebook and Twitter and started talking about what lay ahead and how scared I was. The response was amazing— so many wonderful people offered support and advice and help.

Also, I started talking about having to lose weight for the operation and how I was getting on at WeightWatchers. My meetings were on Wednesdays and I got in the habit of posting my weight loss online on Facebook and Twitter after the meeting. One evening I forgot. I got tied up meeting friends and when I next went online there were dozens of queries on Facebook about why I hadn't posted my weight, and what had happened. Suddenly I realised that hundreds of people were following my progress every week. It was a shock and I wasn't sure how I felt about it at first. But I decided I could tap into their expectation and use it as a boost to help me get a result. I also felt a little responsible for what was now a growing number of people who were apparently drawing from me, as much as I was drawing from them. I didn't want to let them down. When I went to my WeightWatchers classes, I didn't want to let my leader down either, but most importantly, I now didn't want to let ME down. I probably didn't realise it at the time, but I'd ended up with a really good structure and framework for success: a solid foundation, a good support team, expert advisors and a valid cause or reason to succeed. I was still dreading the operation, but at least I was doing all I could to make it easier, to minimise the risks and increase the potential for a good result. Maybe my friend was right in her comment about control? I now felt I had some control back over the situation and increasingly, life felt good.

My mum and dad were amazing during my sickness and my battle to lose weight. Mum, a doting Irish mammy who previously went out of her way to feed me, was now in the supermarket with her reading glasses in hand, studying the ingredients on packets and watching out for low-fat foods for me. They were both in their eighties when I was hospitalised and I'm so sorry for the worry it caused them. Mum was with me when I went back to the consultant and triumphantly declared after five months that I had lost the required 4 stone for my operation. The surgery was scheduled for November, the following month. All of a sudden the date was rushing towards me. It seemed to have happened so quickly and yet this was what I'd been working for since the summer.

Being admitted to hospital was terrifying. Mum and Dad were with me for the pre-op. I didn't admit how I was feeling because I didn't want to worry them, but when they left, I allowed myself to feel the fear and reduced myself to releasing a few selfish, high-drama, self-pitying tears. What if I didn't wake up? What if I died under anaesthetic? Could this be my last mortal, knowing moment on the planet, could this be it? Was this all I was to achieve, ever? Could it be possible that this was it, this was all there was, that the sum total of my life was about living to this point, to end with a whimper? When I had tortured myself in this vein for half an hour or so, I then turned my thoughts to the possibility that I might survive! I pondered the possible pain, imagined the feel of the knife cutting through flesh and muscle, wondered how I could possibly survive with cuts in my skin, imagined what it must be like to have your stomach held together with cold, hard, metal staples, wondered if I'd be able to bear it. Finally and thankfully, the anaesthetic kicked in . . .

Chapter 2
Pain, Depression—and Hope

I woke up in the recovery room after the operation and my first thought was that my back didn't hurt. My second thought was that the anaesthetic must still be working and then quickly followed the thought that if drugs existed that could stop the pain like that, life was definitely worth living. I had expected that my first reaction would be to reach for my belly and find the incisions and check on what the pain levels were going to be. I did that now.

I felt okay. In fact I felt marvellous. I couldn't get away from the wonderful feeling of being pain-free. The stitches were a minor inconvenience, but lying there on the trolley, I couldn't get over the wonderful fact that my back didn't hurt. I was confused and perplexed and kept checking and wondering. It totally took my attention away from my incisions.

I don't really know how to explain how extraordinarily constant the pain had been up to that point. I'm probably still reluctant to talk about it, because for years I felt people were bored by it. For nearly a decade the pain in my back was a constant companion. It never eased, it never intensified, it was just there—all the time, waking, working and sleeping. Waking up in hospital without pain was almost shocking. For hours, then days and even weeks, I kept looking for it, I couldn't trust myself to believe it wasn't there, I was scared that I was somehow fooling myself, that I was imagining that it was gone, that there was a mistake and any moment the waves would come crashing back in around me. But it never returned. This was my modern-day miracle. For months afterwards I would wake up and check—moving slowly, searching out any hint of stiffness, terrified that it was still there, waiting for it to come back and get me. But it never did, it never has, although I'm still a little scared that maybe someday it might. I have as many questions now as then. When I suffered the pain, no one could tell me why—and when it went, no one could tell me why either. There was plenty of speculation; my doctors all in general agree that it was associated with my gall bladder. There was plenty of comment about back pain being associated with gall bladder disease, there were comments about twisted nerves and organs under pressure and various thoughts and impressions, but there were no answers.

My discarded gall bladder was sent for tests and my consultant told me it showed about eight to ten years of chronic disease, which is about the length of time I'd suffered with my back. Who knows and really, who cares? The most important thing for me was that I'd been freed. I walked out the door of the hospital a free woman. Imprisoned for ten years in a body that wouldn't work, I was now rejoining the world. I threw myself into living, the multicoloured joy of being me. I bounced back to the gym and within six weeks I was lifting weights again, redoubling my efforts on the treadmill and losing lots more weight. I joined a new yoga class; I tried a different style this time, called Hatha. It is a gentler discipline which I prefer and which taught me a little more about myself and how to breathe properly, which was later to help me through one of the biggest challenges in my life.

I was back and I was empowered, passionate, focused, and determined to claw back every moment of lost opportunity and missed time. And then I got depressed.

I don't think I've ever suffered depression. I have friends who live life a little up and then a little down, whereas I've always tended to be a happy type of person, even when I was 23 stone and even when I was sore and tired and fed up. But just after the operation, just after my modern-day miracle, just as I was losing weight and should have been bursting with happiness, I woke up one morning and I wasn't. I can't explain why; I just wasn't happy anymore. At this stage I had lost 6 stone—almost a person—and should have been thrilled. But I had 6 stone more to lose to reach my WeightWatchers goal or target weight. I felt I had it all to do again and I wasn't sure if I could do it. It was just before Christmas. I kicked around, huffing and puffing for a day or two, and then I went on Facebook and in an idle moment posted a status update, explaining my dilemma and calling on my new Facebook friends for help. 'Come on FB Friends,' I typed, 'I need inspiration; I've got another mountain to climb!'

I didn't realise it at the time, but among the thousands of people following my progress on Facebook was a lady called Rosaleen Thomas, who worked with The Hope Foundation which supports street kids in Kolkata (Calcutta), India. Rosaleen was attempting to put together a celebrity team to travel to Everest on an expedition led by the renowned Irish adventurer and explorer Pat Falvey. The Foundation was trying to raise awareness about what they do and to raise funds for a new girls' home in Kolkata. After reading my FB appeal, Rosaleen got in touch with me. In an unforgettable phone call she asked me if I *really* wanted a mountain to climb and then invited me to trek with a celebrity group to Base Camp, on Mount Everest.

Some people get excited by mountains and some don't. I didn't even realise that I could have a passion for mountains until that blinding instant. It was my

Eureka, my moment of revelation on my personal road to Damascus. My heart leaped and my breath caught in my throat as for a moment I contemplated getting that close to the highest point on the planet. Then reality set in and I thought of what it meant. I was still around 16 stone and this was a physical challenge that would require superb levels of fitness. Even in my complete ignorance I realised that and yet, what a challenge! What a possibility and what a chance to say thanks to someone or something or some entity or some planet ...

For weeks I'd been relishing my new health and wondering how it had happened and how my years of pain had ended so abruptly and shockingly. I'd been looking around to try and put an explanation to it, to find someone or something to thank, a deity, the universe, something. Now, just a few weeks before Christmas, this charity called 'Hope' had come knocking on my door and asking me to use my newly revived body to help their cause, and I felt I could hear fate knocking too. I knew I wanted to do it, but could I? Would I physically be able to deliver? I didn't want to start something and just give up and let people down halfway through. I wanted to speak to two people: my consultant and the expedition leader, Pat Falvey. Through my work as a journalist I knew of Pat's reputation as a mountaineer and explorer who has conquered Everest's summit twice from north and south, and completed the Seven Summits challenge twice, by climbing the seven highest mountains on the seven continents—then doing them all again! Even now the man was launched on a new adventure to seize the holy grail of explorers, the so-called 'three Poles challenge'—the North Pole, South Pole and Everest. I knew my consultant would offer an expert opinion on what my body was capable of and I knew instinctively that Pat—one of the most experienced expedition leaders in the world—would know whether I had the time to turn myself around before the team was due to leave.

I hit the phone. Not unreasonably my consultant sounded surprised at my inquiry but quickly enough assured me that if I could get myself fit there was no medical reason why I couldn't take on the climb and the high altitude. My lack of a gall bladder and the recent surgery would not be an issue. Then I rang Pat, introduced myself by phone and explained that I'd been approached to join the team he was due to lead. I told him about losing 6 stone, having 6 stone more to lose, the old back pain and eight years of inactivity and how much training I'd need and asked if he thought I'd have enough time to do it. There was a long silence and then Pat's Cork/Kerry accent rang in my ear as he remarked that what I had done was already extraordinary and was 'possibly the reason why I might not make it to Everest Base Camp'.

That stumped me. Why would my achievements work against me? Pat went on to explain that when

the going got tough I might say to myself, 'You've
done well enough, you've done enough.' It was my
turn to pause. 'So you're saying if my head can climb
the mountain, my body will follow,' I said. He didn't
disagree. My next phone call was to Rosaleen—I told
her I was going.

Training now had to take on a whole new meaning,
I realised that. I had a new challenge and a new focus
and time was already running out. The expedition
was due to leave in October, which might seem a long
way down the line, but I was far behind catching up
with even a 'normal' level of fitness, never mind the
super-fitness required for Everest. Part of me realised
I was crazy to attempt it, but I didn't let those
thoughts hang around long in my mind, knowing
that I'd be finished before I started if I allowed them
to get a hold. I was still struggling to walk an incline
for 15 minutes on the treadmill at the gym and I
needed to walk up a mountain for eight hours a day.
The struggle ahead seemed enormous, so I broke it
down and got organising. Looking back, that's
another key lesson I learned. Break it down because
taking one step at a time is manageable. *I couldn't
climb mountains right now, but I could keep putting
one foot in front of the other.*

My first visit was back to the gym, where I spoke
to the manager and explained that I now wanted to
engage a personal fitness trainer. To be honest, when
I explained that it was for a charity challenge and told

them about Everest, I thought they might give me a cut off the cost—they didn't but that's life. I thought about it as an investment in my health as well as a contribution to the challenge, but it was the first of many expenses to come and it was something I really hadn't considered. When you work in a business like radio the common perception is that you're loaded, but I'm afraid I'm a journalist, not a star, and I'm a single girl paying a mortgage so realistically I don't have much cash to splash. It was just one more challenge to stack up against the rest.

The gym team suggested a trainer, but I cut in and explained that it had to be David, because of all the time and attention he'd given me earlier when he made out my fitness instruction programme. All arranged, I trotted down to David and explained that I had a new challenge and that I now needed to lose a lot more weight and go on an expedition to the highest mountain in the world. 'No problem,' said David and off we went again.

The battle had changed now; it was less about weight loss and more about fitness. Rather than fat-burning, I was now to concentrate on growing muscle for strength and endurance. I never ran on the treadmill; I walked, increasing the duration and speed and incline, and then I worked with weights. In particular, David introduced me to kettle bells. Originally developed in Russia, kettle bells are weights that are shaped rather like kettles. They are rounded and have a handle and you can throw them around your body and above your head. You engage your core muscles when you lift them and need several muscle groups working at once to support the action of throwing them around. I loved them, although until I'd learned a bit of technique they kept rolling back and hitting my wrists, so for weeks I was going into work bruised from wrist to elbow and getting funny looks.

David was great as a trainer. He took my challenge so seriously and I'm forever grateful to him. He spent hours poring over the internet for training styles and tips for how to prepare best for the altitude, which would thin the air and rob me of oxygen, and for walking uphill for hours, for days and weeks. He explained that we needed to build stamina rather than speed, and everything in his programme was aimed towards that for the months to come. I had two sessions a week with David and he gave me programmes to follow on my own for the other days of the week. I could not have got ready in time without him; I simply didn't have the expertise or knowledge to get my body toned on my own, in that time-frame. The money for hiring a personal trainer was well spent.

Fellow journalist and friend Kerry Graye took me out in Malahide and we walked along the seafront with her dogs. It was another milestone and the pictures of the day hit Facebook along with other progress reports on how I was getting on. A stroll with your dogs along the seafront may sound simple, but for me it was the first proper walk outside without a cane in years and it was momentous. To walk away from my car and away from a road for an hour in one direction, knowing that I had to turn around and make it back again, was daunting. This was my first expedition, cut with concern that if I couldn't make it, getting me off that beach could be difficult and embarrassing. I imagined how it must be for an ice skater when they push away from the railing they've been clutching and try and make it upright on their skates for the first time without support. That was how far I had to go, from being scared to walk away from my car to walking through Nepal to Base Camp Mount Everest. Was I insane?

The more I planned and longed for Everest, the more scared I got about the challenge that lay ahead and whether I'd be up to the task. I was increasingly intrigued by the effects of high altitude and hungry for information. I watched documentaries and read books, Google searched and asked Pat Falvey lots of probably irritating questions! When you reach high altitude, you're robbed of oxygen and everything becomes more difficult, you struggle to breathe and even bending to tie a shoelace is a major physical event. Walking slowly is an effort, with muscles and lungs screaming at every step. The pressure affects you, and your lungs and brain can swell with fluid. Altitude sickness can develop into a condition called Acute Mountain Sickness. AMS, as it is known, commonly kicks in at around 8,000 ft and can create effects ranging from headaches to flu-like conditions to symptoms resembling a hangover or carbon monoxide poisoning. Some people are affected more than others and there seems to be little way of telling who will be susceptible. It doesn't end there; AMS can progress to high altitude pulmonary edema (HAPE) or high altitude cerebral edema (HACE) which are both potentially fatal. There is no real cure for either, other than to get lower down the mountain and do it quickly.

I read somewhere that swimming was a good exercise for preparing for exertion at high altitude. So I contacted the local Masters Swimming Club at Dublin's new olympic-sized baths, the National Aquatic Centre (NAC) or Bertie Bowl, as it was cheekily dubbed by Dubs, after the former Taoiseach who'd pressed ahead with its construction amid much controversy. I asked if I could join some of their training sessions and these incredibly talented athletes generously permitted the newbie to tag along. I love swimming, but these guys and girls are tough. Their training session involves swimming lengths for a whole hour without stopping, in various styles, in various combinations and at various speeds. I gasped and heaved to keep up, but gradually got better—if not at swimming faster, then certainly at the art of getting out of the way of the group about to lap me, cutting down the lane towards me like a Scud missile. Scary.

Finally it was time to get out on a mountain. Pat Falvey had told us that the most important part of training for Everest was actually getting out on the hills and getting mountain fit. So it was time to get my skates on—or should I say my hiking boots—and take it out there.

There was more unexpected expense and some embarrassment before I could get out onto the Wicklow hills to walk with Rosaleen from Hope, who'd offered to bring me on my first hike. I needed boots, which would set me back around €100, and when I went into the Great Outdoors in Dublin to buy them, I also realised as I looked around at the rails of sports clothes and equipment that I needed the rest of the gear to go with them. It only occurred to me when I walked into the store that I had no walking clothes, no waterproofs or rucksack, nothing. I knew from years of writing and broadcasting news that hill-walkers who take to the mountains without proper gear usually end up in bad situations and I dreaded the prospect of taking a starring role in one of my own news bulletins! I set about the task of buying the requisite three layers for walking: inner, mid and outer. An inner layer that wicks or drives sweat away from the body so that you don't get cold, a fleece to keep you warm and an outer water- and wind-resistant jacket made with Goretex or some similar material that allows sweat out and keeps the rain from getting in. The rucksack is to put layers into as you take them off, which you do when you build up heat during a hike. You also need extra socks, a night light, a survival blanket, a whistle, a map and a compass. Those are just some of the basics for keeping you safe in the hills. You also need food, but particularly water—especially in summer. I needed a set of walking poles too, but I didn't know what they were at that stage.

I tried on fleece after fleece, finding none that would fit. I had a similar problem with the jackets and I cringed with embarrassment as the sales staff tried to help. Sports clothing manufacturers do not in my experience retail for ladies who are as large as I was then. Even though I'd lost a load of weight, I was still morbidly obese, carrying around 5 stone in extra weight, and I simply couldn't get anything to fit. I ended up with xxxl menswear sizes, which swamped my 5-ft frame but matched my girth—at a squeeze. Back at home, I turned up the ends of the trousers and the arms of the jacket and used gaffer tape to keep myself together. It was a farce and I was mortified, but I smothered the thought, slapped on some fake confidence and went online with yet another report for my Facebook and Twitter friends, appearing thrilled with my purchases.

On Saturday morning at 6 a.m. I drove away from my house in Clonsilla, West Dublin, to drive an hour and a half to County Wicklow. Rosaleen and I got our boots laced on in the car park at Glendalough. I'd seen the renowned monastic round tower in tourist books and on postcards but I'd never actually travelled out from the city to see it. I marvelled as I surveyed the beauty of the parkland and forest, the lakes and the mountains reaching up beyond us all around. Rosaleen stretched and did some warm-up exercises and I copied her. We both strapped on our rucksacks and started off towards the lower lake. Rosaleen was walking fast and within minutes I was out of breath. I was nervous too and that also affected my ability to breathe. She looked up towards the green hills that stretched ever higher beyond us and said, 'Would you like to know which one you're climbing or would you prefer not to think about it?' I looked around and thought about that. Looking up, they all looked pretty scary. 'Tell me,' I said. 'That one,' said Rosaleen, pointing off into the distance to the highest peak of all, which I now know as Spink Mountain.

We increased our pace along one of the two famous lakes, which was reflecting the blue of the sky and the dark sharpness of the pines lining its shores. We walked from road to stony path to spongy trail with pine needles cushioning our boots. The smell of herbs and grass and bruised pine cones underfoot was heady. It was cold, there were patches of snow and ice around the edge of the trail after the winter's heavy conditions, but the sun was out and I felt warm. Uncomfortably warm. I kept walking, embarrassed to want to stop, but I was sweating and my face was red and I began to feel nauseous as we started to move towards an incline that would bring us to the zig-zag trail leading to the Miners' Village and beyond. I finally found my voice. 'Hang on,' I called to Rosaleen, 'I need to take something off.' I was shy, out of my depth and intimidated. I now know that taking layers on and off is a normal part of being on a mountain. You need to adjust your temperature as you go along and there's no big deal about that. But if you've been unfit and in particular if you've been fat, you get embarrassed about your fitness and you're outside your comfort zone when you're trying to keep up with others who are fitter than you. Rosaleen had no idea how uncomfortable I was and that was my fault, not hers. *As before, there was help there—I just needed to learn how to ask for it.*

We moved on again and this time, wearing a walking vest in the cold air, I felt much better. It was much easier to move and there was no more overheating but I still found the going tough. We came to the base of the Miners' Village, named after the miners who used to live in Glendalough and mine in the hills that we were now passing underfoot. There was a stream and beautiful pale quartz that glistened in the early March sun. We climbed over stepping stones and reached boulders which we scrambled across, getting to the zig-zags. That's when the real climb began. I huffed and puffed and panted like a carthorse. Every bend in the path was a marker to sit and drink water, to turn back towards the lake we'd now left behind, to admire the view and suck, suck, suck, to get my breath and stop my chest from heaving. It took hours to get to the top. The views were stunning but the walk was hard—for me. Other hillwalkers skipped past us on the route, sides hardly moving and no sense of exertion on their faces. I smiled wanly as they passed and some smiled back. Others were clearly unbothered by the gasping female's attempts at inclusion. I wondered what they thought of me and how unfit I was; did they think I was ridiculous or pathetic or did they think, 'Fair play to her'? I knew it shouldn't bother me, but it did and it was one more thought to hide away for now, even if I dragged it out for further examination later. I was determined I wasn't going to let lack of confidence ruin my chances this time and that meant sometimes stopping my imagination from running away.

We came to a waterfall where a small stream spread out into several cascades and sang loudly and prettily over jagged rocks. It sparkled and danced in the sunlight and my breathing didn't matter for a while. It was drowned out by the sound of the river and the pleasure of being alive. We clambered over some more rocks and reached a bridge across the river which separated the geography and led to a path beyond that inclined up to a darker, stiller place. Spink Mountain lay ahead. We stopped to eat lunch and drink water before moving on to the path marked with railway sleepers that stretched up through boggy headland to the peak of the Spink. It was tough going again. The sleepers were stretched with wire, but traced with frost. They were slippery and they kept going up and up. My breathing was laboured again, my calf muscles moaned, my thighs hurt, my back hurt—sending a familiar shiver of fear up my spine. Was it really better or could this be a sign that the back pain was returning? Cursing my imagination again, I closed Pandora's box and finally we made the last push and pulled up across the top.

'All downhill from here,' said Rosaleen, and it wasn't a moment too soon. She'd been telling stories to pass the time while I'd been grunting yes and supplying the odd laugh to keep things going, totally unable to talk because I needed every whisper to breathe. We didn't stop at the top of Spink but headed down the mountain towards an observation platform a couple of hundred feet below and that's where we came to a halt. The two lakes of Glendalough stretched out below us, the zig-zags, the stream we'd crossed, the rocks we'd clambered over, the car parks and historic Glendalough tower in the distance. 'Look how far you've come,' whispered Rosaleen quietly. The words had a dozen meanings as I looked out across the beautiful, sun-filled valley with its streams and lakes shining in the sun. I felt two worlds collide, I thought of how far I'd come and how far I wanted to go, I thought of eight years trapped on a chair at work and I started to cry.

Chapter 3
To Climb Your Own Mountain

I feel nauseated and claustrophobic and there's a rising sense of panic that is catching my breath and making my heart pound. My stomach is cramping, I'm roasting hot, rivers of sweat are rolling down my face and back and I'm horrified that I'm going to be sick. Not more than 20 minutes ago, I started to hike up my second mountain with a group of strangers and within moments I realised I was totally out of my depth.

Being here on Knockmealdown Mountain is quite an accident.

One week after the Spink, I found myself in Tipperary with friends from a car club. Old cars have long been a love of mine. I drive a 20-year-old MX5 convertible and I belong to a group of roadster owners who keep in touch through an online forum and meet up during summer months to go for long drives at beautiful spots around the country. Full of enthusiasm after my adventure in Wicklow, I was thrilled to discover that one of the drivers was interested in hillwalking and mountaineering. On the spur of the moment, I eagerly accepted an invitation to extend my weekend and go walking the following day. I had a sense of trepidation beforehand when my climbing friend asked if I had walking poles and I caught the concerned glance in his eye when I admitted I not only didn't have any, but didn't know what they were. Shortly afterwards we came across an advert showing that the local Lidl supermarket were doing a special on outdoor sports gear and was selling walking poles, so a quick drive later, walking poles were acquired and I told myself that it was meant to be. It was one of my 'I'll have a go' moments—and it was terrible.

We got out of our cars on a mountain road, stepped into the heather and started up a steep incline that just kept dragging sharply up with no meandering and no warm-up. At this stage I still weighed around 16 stone and my short frame struggled to keep balance as I lifted my legs high to climb over the wild, tough heather that reached half-way up my thigh. I'd already lost sight of my MX5 buddy, who had moved on ahead with the faster climbers, and now my breath laboured as I struggled to keep up with the stragglers. I couldn't believe how quickly I was in trouble, now gasping for breath, my lungs screaming and my legs burning as I pushed to put one foot in front of the other, each time thinking that I'd have to stop and turn around, that I just couldn't go on. I was embarrassed, wondered what it would look like if I wimped out and gave up just minutes after I started. I slowed down to try and get relief from a cramp in my side and one of the walkers dropped back alongside. He looked at me quietly for a moment as I tried to get my breath to tell him I was okay, and then he grinned and told me to take off my clothes! Well, it might sound like a rather inappropriate invitation, but I'd been wearing the three layers I'd been told all hillwalkers need along with a hat and gloves and all my zips and clips tightened fast for good measure. I still hadn't learned the lesson about overheating.

My new friend smiled and helped me get out of some of my gear and pack it in my rucksack, advising me to drink some water and take some deep breaths, commenting with good humour that it helped if I remembered to breathe. He told me to relax, not to worry about catching up with anyone, and then he said something which stayed with me through the months ahead and all the pain and worry that was to follow. 'You've got to climb your own mountain,' he said. The words hit me with a resonance that was to echo through my life like a shockwave. I don't even know my Good Samaritan's name and he probably wasn't trying to be eloquent, but he was. It was a simple statement of fact delivered kindly and plainly and it had a huge impact on me. I gathered myself together, put thoughts of the other climbers out of my mind and concentrated on walking my mountain, putting one step in front of the other. Five hours later, I made it back to the parked car. My legs shook and I could hardly walk. I knew I wouldn't be able to drive back to Dublin that night, so I extended my weekend again, booked another night, got into a hot bath and thought back about the day. I was shattered but I'd done it. I had climbed another mountain.

Back in Dublin I now had a serious physical regime in place for the girl who just a few months earlier told WeightWatchers that she'd 'do the diet but not the walking'. I had two personal fitness sessions with David every week, went to yoga one evening and spent another evening swimming with the NAC Masters. Spink Mountain in Glendalough was becoming central to my training. That first walk took me four hours but I went back every Sunday and worked on cutting the time it took me to get around. I didn't realise it then but I was setting up a really good system: starting with manageable amounts of exercise, then increasing effort and speed and gradually maximising my body's efficiency, getting used to a level of stress and then slowly turning up the difficulty. Nothing that I did was too difficult but it was regular. I timetabled exercise and just turned up, bypassing the element of choice or debate along the way, because if I'd stopped to think about it, I would have skipped out and found some reason why I didn't have the time to train. I never would have done the training at all if I didn't have the extreme goal of joining the team going to Base Camp, but I realised that if I wanted to achieve something that unusual, I had to put in an extraordinary amount of effort, because I had so far to go in terms of fitness. All the other people taking part in the Hope project were fit and athletic, while I had started out morbidly overweight and barely able to walk and had a ridiculous amount of catching up to do. I kept telling myself that if it was just a case of hard work, I was ready to give it a shot, but on dark days, I'd look at the glamorous, fit and healthy people who made up the rest of Team Hope and I'd wonder who I was kidding. I was lining up with the gorgeous young Jenny Kavanagh and George McMahon or 'Mondo', both from 'Fair City', Ireland's big home-produced TV soap opera, with TV presenter and recently lauded boxing enthusiast Rob Ross, and with former naval officer, extreme artist and extremely fit Philip Gray!

The climb around Spink Mountain is a trail that is well laid out and maintained by the OPW and is board walked or paved most of the way around. As a newcomer to hillwalking with no experience of map-reading or navigation, I felt confident that I could walk it on my own without getting myself in trouble and having to waste the time and resources of the

Mountain Rescue teams. So I now started walking Spink or 'The Glendalough Horse Shoe', as it's also known, on my own. Our soon-to-be expedition leader Pat Falvey had said the fastest way to get mountain fit was to 'take it to the hills' and this was my way of doing that. I didn't always have someone around who wanted to walk as badly as I did and no one I knew needed to train as regularly as I did, so I knew I was essentially on my own. I'm not saying this is the best way to train, or whether it's clever or effective or professional—but it worked for me. Wicklow was about an hour and a half's drive away from Dublin and despite my limited navigational skills, I couldn't get lost on the trail. So this became my stomping ground. I would hit Glendalough's monastic round towers on Thursday evening after work, and again on Saturday morning, and again on Sunday.

After several weeks, I tried something new, attempting a 'double' one Sunday morning. I walked around the horseshoe as usual, up past the Miners' Village to the top of Spink Mountain, down the steps past the wood and the Poulanass Waterfall, and then back to the car park. I took a cup of coffee from the tourist catering van, talked myself out of ordering a hamburger and sat down at one of the wooden picnic trestles to drink my coffee and admire the mountains reaching up blue and broody through the woodland that partially hid the upper lake. Then I got up and walked it all again. Eventually I was walking Spink on

Thursday evening and then walking doubles on Saturday and Sunday. Finally I added a couple of pounds of lead to my rucksack and started running the downhill bits. It gave me enormous confidence, because I'd spotted hikers doing that in the early hours of the morning when I first started climbing Spink and I'd wondered then how they could possibly do it. Now I was able to carry it off myself and it reinforced the message that small starts could become bigger events, and I could literally see my body getting stronger and faster every weekend.

With all this time spent treading the boardwalk in Wicklow, you'd imagine I'd have been getting pretty bored and fed up. I kept expecting that to happen myself. But every climb was different, every day I went on the mountain there were new sights to see and new feelings to experience. Sometimes it was the way the sun shone on the stone of the gully, sometimes it was catching sight of an unusually large herd of deer and sometimes it was just my own mood that made the difference. I argued with myself, discussed my diet and plans and hopes and fears. I had cut the time it took me to walk the horseshoe to two hours, but doubling up meant I was out there for four hours at a time. The phone signal was usually blocked out by the mountains, so my iPhone didn't work. It meant that I was unable to engage with the world outside and with the usual distractions of life and work removed, I found that I was connecting more with myself and my own thoughts. It was valuable time and it seemed to generate the same sort of calm that I felt after yoga. On a whim I started repeating some of the yoga exercises at home when I was getting ready for bed and before long I was spending a couple of minutes exercising when I woke up too. I found it gave me a base-line, a small chance to connect with myself each day, which I now think is very valuable in such a busy world.

We are often so busy running around on someone else's timetable that we can lose track of our feelings and our own needs and wants. On the mountain I learned the importance of listening to yourself and deciding what you really want to do. Of course there has to be a balance, but I think if we could learn to listen to ourselves more it would make life much simpler. These days, in difficult situations, I take time to pause and ask myself what I want to do, what it is that I really feel about the problem, and I usually find that the answer is right there in front of me. Before this wonderful journey I wasted a lot of energy soul-searching about the right way to please other people and make them happy. I now believe a person's happiness is usually in their own hands. I don't believe you can make someone happy; they have to do that themselves. You can have a more positive impact, I think, by concentrating on making yourself as happy and optimistic as possible and then others seem to benefit by association, a sort of happiness by osmosis. As I was growing up, my mum would present me with a largely inexhaustible stock of wise sayings, probably passed on by her own mum and other people that she grew up alongside in County Galway. She always rattled them out by rote at suitable moments and one of her favourites was 'Treat others as you would like to be treated yourself.' She never mentioned it, but I think it could be extended to 'Treat yourself as you would like to be treated by others.'

Exercise was now a major part of my day and week and life, but it had started out being an addition to my diet and my diet remained vitally important. I never missed a WeightWatchers meeting and I was still posting updates on Facebook about the weekly weigh-in. It was great to speak to the ladies at the meetings in Dublin 15 and share experiences. I was a little less vocal about all the walking I was doing. I didn't want to make anyone feel uncomfortable, because I remembered that when I first came to class I absolutely hated the idea of having to walk anywhere and at the time I used to feel a bit uncomfortable when members talked about the exercise or walking they had done that week. I was still learning invaluable information about diet and nutrition and what worked for some people and clever ways to arrange the day around eating properly. There was plenty to take from all of the meetings and I grasped the knowledge hungrily.

Everyone's daily life is different and we all have difficulties that affect the way we eat or what choices we make. I think the skill of healthy eating is finding what works for you. When people ask me how I lost lots of weight in a very short time, I often jokingly reply that 'I ate my way to a smaller dress size'. I'm not being smart or making fun, it's actually true. I eat much more now than I did at the start of 2010, but I make healthier choices, I eat regularly and I have changed the proportions of the food on my plate. The tricks include using a small plate, drinking lots of water and snacking on vegetables or fruit, but the principles are simple. Eat small amounts from the high energy food groups with two-thirds of your intake from fruit and veg. If I stick to those principles I lose weight. If I don't—I gain. There are keynote discoveries that I made while actively trying to lose weight. One of the most important things for me is to keep a food diary to note down what I eat and drink each day. I find the actual process of taking account of what I have used during the day is key to my personal success. If I don't put it in the book, I tend to forget I've put it in my mouth and pretty soon the snack attacks start building up. If I don't track properly, I also 'guesstimate' what calories I have consumed and have often been shocked when I sit down to add them up, to discover that I have eaten much more than I intended or realised. It's a basic check on 'food in—food out', like looking at the fuel gauge in your car to make sure you've got enough power on board for the journey.

I also find planning is vital. My WeightWatchers leader, Vera Baker, told me at one of her classes that if I allowed myself to get hungry, I would make bad choices about food. Again it was one of those simple messages that really made an impact. I already knew that if I went to the supermarket when I was hungry, I would buy lots of goodies and once they were in the house I would later track them down and eat them. I think everyone knows that. But what Vera said made me expand that thought a bit further and I realised that it applied to everyday life too. I started trying to make a point of eating every four hours to get ahead of the hunger pangs. When I did that, I found that when it came to having my meal I was perfectly happy with the portions and ingredients I'd prepared. On the other hand, if I missed a meal and I was hungry, I'd eat my lunch or dinner—but still feel unsatisfied and end up going for round two. It was as if my brain took a long time to get rid of the 'hungry' message. It seems really simplistic, but it made a difference for me. I'd drop an apple or a banana in my handbag in case I missed a meal or work ran late and a banana was also a good fallback if I was running late in the morning and was tempted to miss breakfast. I eventually came to the conclusion that bringing breakfast to work was the best arrangement for me, because I was always tempted to spend another 10 minutes in bed and then ended up running for the door. So last thing at night I started to prepare my breakfast and packed lunch for the next day. Typically breakfast would be 30 g of cereal with a handful of blueberries in a plastic box, with a tub of low-fat yogurt on the side. Lunch box number two would have salad with some meat or fish and a slice of brown bread in it. Salad doesn't need to be boring; I'd add olives and fresh beetroot and chopped peppers and cherry tomatoes, raw mushroom, seeds or nuts, perhaps raisins and maybe other fruit. I'd also use a lo-cal salad dressing, or a squeeze of orange or lime or lemon and some herbs or sweet chilli sauce.

I discovered a whole host of stunning new flavours that don't need high-fat or high-chemical additives to make a taste sensation. Planning meals in advance meant I spent less time thinking about what I was going to eat, because it was more or less arranged from the day before, and that stopped me making poor choices while running around stressed and hungry. It's about finding what works for you, and running with it. My weight loss adventure has become a voyage of discovery, finding new tastes and culinary wonders that I never dreamed possible. Strawberries and cracked black pepper with smoked salmon? Who knows? Throw it together and experiment. People look at a fat person and presume they have a love affair with food, but I used to feel I hated food. I felt I was addicted to something; but I couldn't avoid temptation by cutting it completely because we all need food to survive. Drug addicts and alcoholics can, with strength, walk away from their demon. If you have an unhealthy relationship with food, you've got to learn to live alongside it. It was a conundrum, a chicken and egg, a puzzle, and it felt deeply unfair. Eating is a human function, the most natural thing in the world, but when I was 23 stone I felt I needed to eat in secret. I wouldn't enjoy eating dinner in public and would watch someone watching me and wonder what they were thinking about me. I'd never be seen eating a packet of crisps or a bar of chocolate. But I ate them alone, feeling at the same time that I was horribly sad and totally out of control. I never felt that way about food before I put on all the extra weight and, as I changed my eating habits, those feelings changed and I started to see food again as fuel in and fuel out. When that started to happen, I lost the horrid senseless feelings of guilt and allowed myself to start enjoying food again. I didn't realise it at the time, but looking back, it was as if a huge pressure bubble had burst and there was a massive sense of relief.

Writing these words now, I'm still overweight. I'm 11 stone and size 14 and I have one stone more to lose to reach my target weight. I'm confident of getting there and I'm not afraid of losing too much, as many people have suggested to me, some from genuine concern and some, perhaps, for other reasons. My next battle will be maintenance. I'm worried, of course, that I won't hold it. So many dieters I have spoken to have stories to tell of losing large amounts of weight and then putting it all back on. Obviously I do not want that to happen and am determined it will not, but many people before me have had the same determination only to find they have slipped back to old ways and habits. I think it will be important to keep tracking food intakes and continue to keep a record of fuel in and fuel out and I think I will continue to go to meetings to keep in touch with the ladies who helped me get this far. I've never left one of those meetings without a spring in my step, so I won't consider that a hardship. Perhaps the 'before and after' pictures should stay on the fridge door. Above all, I hope that I now have the knowledge to recognise if I run off the rails and the newly found self-confidence to put a halt to any slide before depression and habit take over again.

At the moment, still actively trying to lose weight, I find that there are a number of hot-spots that affect me badly. I drink around 2 litres of water each day and if I stop that, my weight-loss slows. It also goes south if I snack, if I have too many meals out, if I drink alcohol several nights in a row, or if I eat a lot of processed food. I don't think eating out is necessarily bad; it's just that it's harder to know what you're eating when someone else is cooking. You can't accurately guess the weight of the meat or pasta on your plate, whether there is butter on the veg or not, whether the waitress actually used low-fat milk or maybe forgot. I find you can get away with eating out once or twice a week, but any more than that and the lack of accuracy becomes an issue. Remember I'm talking about actively losing weight here, not living a 'normal' life of maintaining weight at a certain level. People say successful weight loss needs to be a change of lifestyle rather than a change of diet and I agree with that. But I also believe that losing a lot of weight over a lengthy period of time is an unusual condition for the body and mind to be in and I think it's unhelpful to pretend otherwise. I think it's wrong to tell people it's easy to lose weight: it's actually annoying and tough and it's worse if you think that everyone else can do it except you. The truth is that losing weight is a job, but it's totally achievable and within everyone's power once you know what you're up against. You can make it a little easier, but you cannot alter the fact that you need to consume fewer high-energy foods, and eat less of certain types of foods. Exercise helps to tone your body and fine-tune your metabolism, but my personal experience shows that exercise alone will not make you lose weight; you've got to change the quality and quantity of what you put in your mouth.

How can a girl who weighs 8 stone turn into a woman who weighs almost three times that? I did it by eating slightly more than I needed over a long period of time. I lost 12 stone in just over a year by eating slightly less than I needed over a long period of time. I won't insult anyone with weight issues by suggesting that it is an easy road to follow. It's hard, it's unpleasant and uncomfortable and if you decide to do it, you need to put your shoulder to the wheel and keep pushing. The rewards are worth it but you need to keep clear reminders around you to ensure you don't forget why you are in the fight. Photographs on the fridge door, dresses or jeans in a smaller size left on a hanger on your bedroom door, a present of a spa treatment when you lose a stone: use whichever incentive works for you—or use them all. Anything that helps, do it. I had slips and mistakes and bad days and even bad weeks, I still do. You won't win every battle but you won't lose the war as long as you keep going. Most importantly, you have to lose weight because you want to. Not because someone feels you should, or you want to please someone else. It has to be your own choice, or else it simply won't be worth the struggle. You have to want it badly enough to keep strong when you want to give up. I can't stress enough the importance of not giving up and not giving in. I can't count the number of times when I dropped the baton, pigged out, lost discipline and self-control and didn't respect myself in the morning! But you've got to brush off the disappointment of slipping back a bit, get up and put your shoulder back on the wheel. Another lesson: *You can't fail if you're still trying . . .*

The dreaded 'plateaux' hit me too along the way. With all the weight loss success that I had at the start and with all the exercise I subsequently ended up doing, you'd think I would have skipped the maddening frustration of eating well for weeks without seeing a difference on the scale—wrong. For over a month I kept going along to my WeightWatchers weigh-ins and getting on the scale to see no change. It was annoying and really disappointing. Eventually my leader one evening took me aside and just told me to relax. 'This is not your final weight,' she said. 'It will change, this is not the weight you will remain forever. Relax and take it easy on yourself.' I've heard of links between stress and weight gain and perhaps this proves a point, but the following week I chalked up a 2 lb loss. What saved me from giving up during those bad weeks was staying for the meeting afterwards. I still can't fully explain why I always left in good humour, but along with a fresh round of hints and tips from other members' personal experiences, I think it was the reassurance I got that I wasn't alone or unusual. I got great support in the knowledge that so many lovely, clever, talented and powerful women—and men— were stuck in the same damn boat as me. I left each time with a fresh sense of determination that I was going to get on top of this problem and I wasn't going to lose out on the rewards.

For me, the rewards were initially about being alive and having my operation. I don't think I ever would have had the strength to get up and start eating into that 23 stone if a doctor hadn't told me I was too large for that vital surgery I needed to remove my gall bladder. Just imagine being told rather insensitively by a surgeon that 'there wasn't an instrument created that could reach through the fat' that surrounded this important organ, a gland that regulated bile and helped my body to digest fat. I hardly knew what a gall bladder was, had to google it to find out that I could live healthily without it—if, at my weight, I survived the surgery. I was really scared and it was enough to make a difference, to tip the balance of what was more important, losing weight or continuing to comfort eat and let the fat win. Afterwards, when I'd lost that first 4 stone and had my operation, I was so thrilled to feel well and be without pain that I wanted to keep going. I didn't have far to look for reasons to keep fighting and it wasn't anything to do with climbing mountains. I wanted to feel good, to look good, to rejoin life again, to look at an attractive man and harbour the suspicion that he might actually find me attractive too. I wanted to wear pretty dresses, to fit into jeans, to wear high heels without my feet flowing over the sides; simple, ordinary, wonderful things, which already seemed within my grasp.

After losing 6 stone, my body was definitely shrinking and changing. I knew I still had a long road ahead but people were now smiling and complimenting me on how I looked and that felt good. I was going to a gym, using the stairs instead of always waiting for the lift, and I was actually able to walk up a hill. These were things that a few months ago I couldn't even imagine doing. To be honest, a few months earlier, these were things I didn't WANT to do; in fact you wouldn't have caught me walking to the shop. Going to Nepal was not something I had ever dreamed about and it's not what made me lose weight. For me, the trip to Nepal was always a spiritual connection. I strongly felt that I owed the planet a debt of gratitude, and somehow I felt this journey to Everest was a kind of pilgrimage to show in some way that I appreciated life's gifts. It's something that suddenly became a possibility after I lost weight and the sheer impossibility of someone like me doing it proves what the human spirit is capable of. I'm not an athlete, I'm not a sexy young girl with an hourglass figure, I'm an overweight woman of 45 who has lost 12 stone and climbed to Base Camp Mount Everest and further, to a technical climb hanging off an icy headwall over 20,000 ft high at Island Peak. How is that possible?

I'm not arrogant and I'm not stupid. I know climbing mountains isn't everyone's ideal or aspiration and I'm aware that what happened to me was unusual to say the least. I'm eternally grateful for the incredible things that happened to me on my journey and to the people who inspired and motivated me and helped me to climb my own mountain. I'm not the first person in the world to lose a lot of weight and I won't be the last, but I'm sure one common denominator between us is that we all have our own personal mountain to climb. Our expedition leader Pat Falvey struck a chord with me when I first heard him giving a motivational speech to a business conference in Dublin; he said success in life is about wanting something, believing you can have it and wanting it enough to make it happen. I thought he nailed it and it was another of those life lessons lit up in lights. *Right now, this moment, what do you want? Do you want it bad enough to take it? Then get out there and grab it.*

Chapter 4
Moving Mountains

My dad is 85. He's an amazing man, fit and active, needing no medication despite his age, with a hunger for politics and sport and a passion for his garden which keeps him occupied all year round, particularly during the summer months, when he's missing from dawn until well after dusk. Both I and my mum, aged 82, had long given up pondering what gardening feats could be achieved in a garden in the pitch black of night, but Dad still managed to find something to keep him busy outside until the latest hour. He's always been a man of few words, but that has changed recently for many reasons. A couple of weeks ago he shocked me, admitting that both he and Mum had been preparing for my death, accepting that with my health problems and weight it was likely that I would not survive them. I'm eternally sorry for putting them through that.

As I accelerated my training and started walking on hills, I wondered what both Mum and Dad thought of the changes that were underway and what they understood about my challenge to travel to Everest. I didn't want to concern them and I downplayed my activity, but I wondered if they realised the enormity of the journey ahead. My parents lived with me and one weekend morning at breakfast my dad sat reading his newspaper at the kitchen table, caught in a sunbeam with his legs crossed, the paper held up in front of him and his reading glasses perched roughly halfway down his nose. Slowly and without warning he cast his eyes up above the frame of his lenses and looked at me directly. 'So,' he said dryly, 'if you were to climb Carrauntoohil, Ireland's highest mountain, you'd only have around 17,000 ft to go,' then re-absorbed himself in his paper before I could respond.

So he got it, I thought and then I realised I got it too. I'd have to climb Carrauntoohil and the thought terrified me. For a moment I refused to think about the snow and ice of the lofty heights of the Himalayas and concentrated instead on Kerry and Ireland's highest peaks. If that mountain in Tipperary had pounded me so brutally, how could I ever aspire to climbing Carrauntoohil? I thought again about Knockmealdown Mountain, which I'd later nicknamed 'knock-me-down', and rationalised whether I'd be able to make a better attempt at it now, having several more weeks of climbing the Spink under my belt. I doubted it. I was still breathless and exhausted each time I climbed the Spink, although I was definitely building strength and speed and my breathing was beginning to improve a little. I started wondering about my training and whether I was doing enough, or if I was wildly misguided. Perhaps I needed to be doing much more? Perhaps I was training in completely the wrong way? Perhaps I would never be able to realise my ambition and would end up making a fool of myself on a mountain far away from home. Perhaps I would slow down the team, disappoint my parents and everyone who was beginning to put faith in me and, worse, disappoint myself? I went online and searched for accounts of Carrauntoohil and stories about people who had climbed it. There were many streams of information on the Internet, documenting the severity of the climb, the different routes, water damage and stories of people who have been injured and died. There were warnings from Kerry Mountain Rescue about being responsible on a mountain and ensuring you were well informed and well equipped to be on it. There were lots of stories and lots of reports and I found it all terrifying. Against all this debate and research and thought was the underlying certainty that there was no avoiding this mountain. If I wanted to aspire to

Everest then there was no question that I had to be able to climb the biggest peak at home.

The Hope Foundation and expedition leader Pat Falvey had specified that training and assessment at Pat's Mountain Lodge in Killarney and a climb on Carrauntoohil were necessary requirements for the team that would finally qualify to go out to Nepal. Pat would not agree to take anyone on the trip who had not reached a satisfactory level as decided by him and his staff. I welcomed that. In fact I was relieved that at least if I did my best and my best was not good enough, there was a safety net that would prevent my ignorance from putting myself and others in danger. I trusted Pat and his team and as a journalist I had been aware of his amazing adventures around the world, never thinking that I might one day get a taste of that extreme environment myself. The growing problem now for me was time; I was in a race against my own body. The months were disappearing and I had so little time to travel such a long way in terms of fitness and strength. I needed a measure to judge my improvement and judge if I was going to have enough time to make it. The first training weekend in Kerry kept being put back because the celebrity group was having difficulty getting their diaries to match on free time. Fundraising events were now also occurring and eating into the weekends that were available for training. I felt I was losing control, felt frustrated that I was losing time and valuable opportunities for assessment by someone who understood about putting expeditions together and the human requirements that were needed.

Finally, I picked up the phone to Pat and asked straight out if I could make a solo visit to the Lodge and impose on his experience to judge my fitness. I explained I was happy and willing to come down on the official weekends when they were decided, but felt I needed advice sooner than that and I cheekily asked whether I could 'come and climb his mountain'. Pat responded without missing a beat and asked what I was doing that weekend. I'm still not sure if that was a specific challenge but I responded in kind and answered that I was flying down to Kerry. Pat paused before breaking into laughter and went on to offer me the hospitality of his Mountain Lodge in Beaufort near Killarney and I got off the phone and booked my flight.

Sitting on the small Aer Arann plane en route to Tralee, I had time to pause and ponder the moment. I wanted and needed this experience, but when it came, I realised I hadn't expected it quite so quickly. Ideally, I would have liked another week of pushing myself on the Spink before setting off to take on Kerry's lofty heights. But after asking such an experienced mountaineer to give up his time and energy to take me out on the hills, I could hardly start backtracking and whimpering about timings. I had to go for it. As the demons continued to poke me, I suddenly thought about staying on my own at the Lodge. I had never thought to ask whether there were other strangers staying there or whether I was actually walking into someone's home. Perhaps I was really imposing on this man and being appallingly forward. Perhaps this man thought I was incredibly stupid or worse—a single woman travelling down to spend a weekend in the home of a man she had never met. I know, stupid thoughts, but I told you the demons were prodding me and I would not be entirely honest if I didn't admit that my imagination took flight. We landed at the airport and I followed my instructions to get a taxi to Beaufort and Kate Kearney's Cottage. We were halfway there and I was explaining to the driver that I was going to Pat Falvey, who lived in a Mountain Lodge near Kate's, and thankfully the driver knew where I was going. He told me that everyone around knew about Pat and his adventures, he called him 'the King of Kerry' and said that I'd never have any problem trying to find him. Not bad for a Corkman!

Suddenly, as we were approaching Killarney, my mobile rang and a staff member at Tralee Airport inquired if I'd left a set of walking poles behind. I was distraught. I badly needed the poles to walk because they took up to sixty per cent of the pressure from my knees, which I was still trying to strengthen, and I knew I wouldn't make it up Carrauntoohil without them. I was sure Pat would have poles at the Lodge, but was loath to arrive down from Dublin, a bumbling newbie who didn't even have the right equipment with her. Because the walking poles were pointed, the airline had put them in the airplane hold at Dublin and with my flight of fancy taking off as it did on the way to Tralee, I was quite distracted and had completely forgotten about them on arrival. I could have kicked myself. There was no option only to tell the cabbie to swing around and head back to the airport to retrieve them and fess up to Pat that I was going to be late. I'd already phoned him on arrival, so it was a bit of an embarrassing start to ring back and explain I'd had a 'd'oh' moment. But I knew it would pass quickly. Returning the way we had come a few minutes earlier, I had time to reflect on how nice the airport was to contact me and marvel at how they knew the sticks were mine and where they got my mobile number. Of course it was all on the luggage barcode, I suppose, but all the same it was razor sharp and great service. On arriving at the airport, the lass who had rung me was actually standing outside the airport building and waiting for me with poles in hand—now that's really above and beyond the call of duty. When I stopped to thank her and express my surprise, she said she knew I'd probably be heading into the hills for the weekend and didn't want me to miss out. What a lovely young woman and what a massive vote of confidence in Tralee Airport and Irish courtesy and kindness. Ireland rocks!

Turning off the road in Beaufort beyond Kate Kearney's Cottage, I was bumped into a new sense of realisation. We were on a very rough laneway, virtually a dirt track, heading sharply upwards into the hills. I'd already felt apprehension as we approached Beaufort with the ring of mountains closing in around me and blocking out the moon with their height, and now as we left the smooth tarmac of the national road behind, I again realised I was taking on an entity I'd never encountered before. The mountains seemed to have their own pulse, seemed to be watching me as I got closer, holding back their observations with a baleful eye, content to see how I'd engage with them. I had no doubt whatsoever that their patient watchfulness could change in a heartbeat to something much more animated and malevolent. Imagination taking flight again, I admitted to myself that I was simply nervous about meeting Pat and downright scared about climbing the next day. Pat had told me on the phone when I'd touched down that there would be a group going out and while I was relieved that I'd have company, I was also worried that I wouldn't keep up—or worse, that I'd slow them down.

We found the Lodge; I paid the driver and walked around to the front door of the charming stone building, liking it instantly with that strange connection that we sometimes make with houses and places. I don't know if that's a universal condition or some Irish sensitivity, perhaps developed through years of listening to tales and stories at our mothers' knees. At least that was my experience of growing up, with yarns galore mixing culture with fairies in a kaleidoscopic tapestry of sound and colour. I love the feeling of being part of something ancient. Anyway, my rush of warmth for Beaufort and the Lodge didn't lessen my apprehension as I knocked on the door and shortly introduced myself to Pat and his friend Gerry, who was also going to be guiding us and who lives in the purple house he built next door! Characters both, they charmed me from the moment I stepped into the circle of light that beamed from Pat's hall—a shrine to explorations and expeditions past and present.

Sitting in Pat's lounge with the two men chatting about politics and sport, I relaxed for a while and tried to get a grip on my surroundings. All around me the Irish greats of climbing looked down from the walls, with Pat's portrait among them, pain etched in those faces from the cold reality of battling Mother Nature in some of the most extreme environments on the planet. I got a couple of history lessons from the lads and we chatted long and hard. I curled up in front of the fire and enjoyed getting to know these two men, enjoying their stories and the easy camaraderie of what was clearly a long friendship. These two old dogs had spent many a long night barking together and I liked them both. I knew the night was disappearing quickly and I was loath to see it go, knowing the day ahead was likely to be among the hardest I'd ever known, physically and probably mentally too. Eventually conversation switched to the mountain. I asked about the group going out, probing and trying to determine exactly how out of my depth I was. There was a mixed group of climbers apparently, a couple who had hillwalked for years, and a group of work colleagues from Cork, one of whom ran marathons for a hobby. I explained what I had been doing in training and that I needed to assess how much I had achieved and how much more was needed. I was wary about making excuses, didn't want to prejudice tomorrow's climb by a certainty of failure, but I genuinely wanted to put the two men in the picture about what I knew I was capable of and what I thought I might be able to handle. Gerry was also going to be guiding us. We ran through a checklist of my gear and then Pat, quite circumspect, put the role of charming host to one side and spoke clearly and minimally about the needs of the moment. 'There may come a point on the mountain when I tell you to move—and then you must move,' he said, 'when timing becomes a matter of safety on a mountain and there's nothing personal about it.'

I looked Pat straight in the eye and said, 'If you tell me to move, I'll move.' But inside I quaked. What if I wasn't able to? There were so many unanswered questions in my mind. I was terrified, I was completely out of my depth, these people were going to waltz up this mountain and I was going to fail, I could taste the disappointment and feel the cringing embarrassment wash around me. Enough. I kicked the demons into touch and stopped the flight of fancy, lecturing myself to stop being stupid, knowing that if I let myself think I was going to fail, I was probably going to fail. I forced myself to focus on the advice from the unnamed man on a mountain in Tipperary. I would climb my own mountain, not Pat's or Gerry's or a marathon runner's. I would do it my way, I would do it one step at a time, one foot in front of the other—and I would do it.

Next morning I was sick. I awoke with my stomach in knots, with cramping and multiple trips to the toilet. I wasn't concerned—not about this. When I danced as a child I always felt like this before a competition, and I knew it was just nerves, and I knew it would pass. I headed to the kitchen and there were hugs all around, which was nice. I'm tactile and I like hugs; they make me feel at one with the world. There were people dropping in and out in various stages of mountain dress, heavy thick socks and gaiters and cool climbing gear, professional-looking fleeces and great happy smiles as Jeeps and four-wheel drives pulled up outside and people tumbled out. Everyone seemed to know what they were doing and I played the part. Pat made me porridge. Porridge is my dad's choice of breakfast, but I'd never eaten it before—never wanted to! But Pat told me it was a slow release carbohydrate and perfect for keeping energy going on a mountain so I did as I was told and cleared the bowl. It wasn't great, but it wasn't bad and it gave me something to do. I'd explained my fitness level last night and I wasn't going to bring it up again or court sympathy or reassurance. There were clearly paying customers on this group and I wasn't going to be the weak link after accepting Pat and Gerry's hospitality, so I slapped on a confident face and tied on my hiking boots. In a screech of tyres and a crunch of gravel, we were off. Three cars loaded up and headed for Cronin's Yard, the by now legendary rest-stop, café and car park at the foot of Carrauntoohil.

Speaking later about my first visit to the highest mountain in Ireland, Pat admitted that he had taken one look at me the night before and decided there was little chance that I would make it up. 'At this stage I thought she was huge and from a health point of view I worried that she wouldn't make it. I was actually concerned that she might be at risk of a heart attack attempting the climb—the other people I was guiding that day looked fit and this was a strenuous day out that was being planned. However, by the time we had finished, she had out-climbed the other people on the hill. It surprised me, which enabled me to think she could go on and do anything she wanted to do.'

I'm deeply indebted to Pat that he was willing to let me try. It was one of the most extraordinary days that I'd ever had the pleasure of experiencing. It was scary, tough, challenging and totally unique. I love that mountain and always will. I made it to the top and couldn't wait to tell my dad, feeling his ironic comment at breakfast a month previous had given me the spark to take it on. As soon as I got back to Cronin's Yard I jotted down the thoughts that I'd experienced and later made a YouTube video for my Facebook page with the words flowing easily over the pictures in my mind.

Voiceover from Teena's YouTube video

Pushing over the top of the ridge I gasp in surprise, 'You kept this a secret,' as the grey slatted rocks that I'd been climbing up like stairs fell away to a ridge that slipped over the edge of the world. With green and grey and golden waves, rolling off into the clouds below to crash on rocks as old as the world itself.

Arriving at the Mountain Lodge of adventurer Pat Falvey, I wear my enthusiasm for the climb ahead like a badge or a suit of armour, as quaking in my climbing boots, I wonder if I really can make it to the top of Carrauntoohil, at 3,500 ft Ireland's highest mountain. I dread the thought of slowing down the group heading out. Is walking in the Wicklow Hills enough preparation or I will I be hopelessly outpaced and mortified in front of strangers? Listening carefully to the brief beforehand, I spot the change of tone as the larger-than-life Pat switches gear from wisecracks and fun to sober comment, host turned leader as he talks about the need to keep up when push comes to shove. There are only so many hours of daylight to climb a mountain. Another snatched, silent conversation with myself as I consider what now seems like the lunacy of being here. I breathe deeply, commit myself, and we're off.

Walking past the memorials in the car park at the foot of Carrauntoohil, I'm reminded that we're approaching a sleeping giant, sweeping calmly up in front, glowing green and purple, serene in the sun, but ready with a fickle flick to change the odds in a heartbeat. Crossing the first of a number of bridges on our way up, our guides explain about flash floods that ran off the mountain, snatching the life from one young woman within sight of the very car park we had just left. It's sobering. But we push ahead, and despite being nervous, my spirits soar as my muscles warm and I break into a light sweat, learning more about the other climbers in the group and feeling relief as I discover that I'm not the only one here for the first time. There's huge reassurance in that and company for the challenge ahead.

Approaching the first of three lakes, we stop to catch our breath and catch up on more from the guides about the history and folklore of the hills around us. Shortly afterwards we come to a halt at what, to me, is an impenetrable sheet of rock. 'Three points of contact, up,' cries Pat, explaining briefly that two arms and a leg, or two legs and one arm—three limbs in total—must be connecting with the mountain at all times. Then he is up and climbing. No ropes, no clips, no carabiners, no dress-rehearsal, no way. 'Are you mad?' I scream silently to myself, toying with the thought of running as fast as my climbing boots would take me in the opposite direction. Breathing deeply, another silent conversation with myself, I call on my personal mantra for tough times, 'One foot in front of the other and breathe.' I focus, find the foothold Pat points to and looking up, the rocks above begin to take on new images of handholds and potential grips. Swinging up to my three points of contact, I look again, and seek and find and reach and stretch and find my feet. My confidence growing, I move again, switching weight, muscles engaging, reacting, responding. My breath deepens and I find a rhythm. I'm scrambling, and a smile bursts across my face as I realise I'm loving it.

A couple of hours later, after climbing over rocks, picking through moss and heather and the trudge of putting one foot in front of the other on tired legs, the seasons change again and bright sunshine gives way to a biting, icy rain and a piercing wind. As the elements kick off I rip out fleece and coat and hat and gloves. How quickly a warm body can change to deathly chill on a mountain, a chilling nudge from the idle giant. Measured breathing and a steady pace allow for conversation with my colleagues. It's nice, they're good people and we exchange tips about breathing and walking and I learn small, subtle things that make sense on a mountain.

The mist closes in as we close in on the summit. The light is creamy, silver and unusual. With the dark rocks below my feet and hands and the rain dripping from my nose and hair, and stinging my eyes, I feel like I'm walking in a plastic bubble, that I can reach up and punch through to the daylight outside. I'm conscious again of the flow of my breath, of keeping a rhythm, of putting one foot in front of the other. Then a cross looms out of the mist and the wind whips my face as I recognise the scene from photos pored over in recent days. We've made it. I've made it.

Standing at the top, hugging, laughing, sharing smiles and joy with other climbers coming over the edge, I'm humbled and proud; conflicted and torn between the contradiction of the power of the mountain beneath me and the power of the body that brought me to stand on top of the highest peak in Ireland. Without warning the mist clears, I'm bathed in sunlight, and a sudden movement pulls my eye down off the peak to the rocks below. Clouds are flying past at speed below me, and I wonder in amazement as I watch, feeling slightly dizzy, as if someone put the world on fast-forward.

The descent is tough, weight thrown down on my haunches, but knees and ankles bear up and nothing can wipe the smile from my face. Buzzing, hooked, and knowing it's just the start of new adventures and challenges. Carrauntoohil hasn't seen the last of me, and I have not seen the last of it. In the weeks ahead, working in the gym, grappling with the final few minutes on the treadmill, or groaning over floor exercises, this Kerry mountain will be flashing through my mind: a reward and a promise and a lure to pull that extra mile from the rowing machine. That peak, that feeling of reaching the summit has left Kerry and travelled back to Dublin with me on my journey. Today I have moved mountains.

Chapter 5
Hopes for a Red Dress

It's March and there's a buzz in the air for The Hope Foundation. They are planning their annual fundraising ball and I'm looking forward to going and meeting the rest of the team for the first time. I'm excited but I'm also nervous. These people are celebrities and maybe they might not be the easiest characters to get along with. I'm going to spend three weeks with them in Nepal and I'm the obvious lame duck. I'm not sure how that is going to feel or how I am going to feel about it when I get there. It is a long way to go and a long length of time to be with someone in harsh and limited conditions, so I hope we all get on and I hope I don't slow everyone down too much and make an idiot of myself.

When I look at the difference between myself and the rest of the team it makes the whole project look

At St Anthony's School in
Dulwich, London.

First time to ride at
Chessington Zoo, London.

Photoshoot for World Environment Day 1992, St Stephen's Green, Dublin: Teena (*left*) with Liz McNally from 98FM. (*Courtesy 98FM*)

In the 1980s, 'super pirates' dominated the Dublin radio scene before the introduction of licensed commercial radio. Here Teena reads for the then Q-102.

On holiday in Grand Canaria.

Broadcaster Breffni Clack (*left*) with Teena. 'Sinning' is more fun when it's shared . . .

PPI Radio Awards: 98FM, Station of the Year 2008. (© *Jason Clarke Photography*)

Publicity shot for 98FM.

Recognition of 'services to journalism', with President Mary McAleese and Dr Martin McAleese, October 2007. (*Courtesy of Maxwell Photography*)

Kettlebell stand-off with personal trainer David Dunne. (*Courtesy of Dave Dunne*)

Reaching new heights: on the climbing wall at Trinity College, Dublin.

Fixed rope training for Island Peak in Nepal, with Everest colleague Ed 'Doc' O'Donnell. (*Courtesy of Ed O'Donnell*)

Hiking at Spink Mountain in County Wicklow. Large sizes for hiking gear are hard to come by!

Training for the Rehab Swimathon at DCU. (*Left to right*): DCU trainer Deirdre Mullen, Channel swimmer Fergal Somerville, Anne Morrissey, Teena. (*Courtesy of Rehab*)

Deep in a gully in Carrauntoohil, Co. Kerry, Ireland's highest mountain. (*Courtesy of Pat Falvey*)

'On the beat' for the Cannonball Run, raising funds for Barretstown Kids Camp in County Kildare. (*Courtesy of the Cannonball Run*)

Celebrating a special birthday with a 10-kilometre 'Run for a Life' for the Irish Kidney Association. (*Courtesy of the Irish Kidney Association*)

Abseiling down the 'Wheel of Dublin' at The Point Village, Dublin . . . is it too late to mention I'm afraid of heights? (© *Collins Agency*)

My Howth Coast Guard helpers for the Hope Challenge 2010, raising funds for street children in Kolkata. (*Left to right*): Stephen O'Gara, Gareth Collier, Fergus Cooney, Donnchadh Mac Cobb, Keith Plummer and Declan Howard. (*Courtesy of The Hope Foundation*)

On the hike to Base Camp Mount Everest, with Irish and worldwide adventurer Pat Falvey. (*Courtesy of Pat Falvey*)

In the shadow of the Khumbo: the Hope/Everest team of 2010. (*Courtesy of Ed O'Donnell*)

Girl power en route to Base Camp Mount Everest. Jenny Kavanagh (*back*), Vivian Harrison (*middle*), and Teena (*front*). (© *Hugh Chaloner*)

One foot in front of the other: Teena's trek to Island Peak. (© *Hugh Chaloner*)

Teena with Pat Falvey and Nima Tenji Sherpa, on the summit of Island Peak. (*Courtesy of Mark Orr*)

'I've done it!' Abseiling back down from 20,305 ft Island Peak. (© *Hugh Chaloner*)

My first new dress: Kinsale, Co. Cork.

Mixing it up—back at base for 98FM. (*Courtesy of Richie Buttle Photography, www.richie.ie*)

so much scarier. There's the extreme artist Philip Gray, ex-Navy and built like a tank, who has already climbed on ice and travelled to Nepal and Everest. Ed O'Donnell is on the support side, a scout leader for years who's represented Ireland in outdoor navigation in snow and ice. There's the gifted photographer Hugh Chaloner who has climbed with Ed already on Kilimanjaro. I reckon all three of these lads are well over 6 ft and strong as horses. Rosaleen Thomas from Hope is coming too; she's spent years travelling to Nepal and walking in the Himalayas, she's fit and lives in Wicklow where she's walked the hills for years. There's the young and fit George McMahon who is Mondo in 'Fair City' and everyone's darling, and the beautiful Jenny Kavanagh, who played Cleo in 'Fair City'; she's a trained dancer, thin as a whip and has the natural fitness of youth. There's also Rob Ross, RTÉ presenter and sports fitness fanatic, who's got triathlons under his belt and recently finished a TV series in which he trained and fought as a boxer—and there's me, an overweight woman in her forties who has just stood on a mountain for the first time in her life.

When I break it down like that I get depressed and it all seems so impossible. But I know I won't achieve anything if I let the terrors take over. I've got to trust in myself to do enough work to get me to Nepal and maybe to Base Camp and trust in Pat, who's told me it's possible, and Dave back in the gym, who's told me it's 'no problem'. All the same, even while I'm lecturing myself about the need for a positive attitude, I'm still painfully aware that I'm the odd one out. We are all about to head off to a ball where we will be in the spotlight with cameras and photographers in attendance and I'm going to come up short in the looks department against this lot of lovelies. This is a bit of a gamble because I could end up looking like a complete twit. I'm a journalist, I've written those headlines!

I may not have met the full team yet, but Rosaleen and I are in constant contact and she's excitedly telling me about her dress for the night of the Hope Ball. It makes me stop and wonder about what I'm going to wear. Clothes have been a bit of an issue for the past few months. I've been losing weight for so long and so quickly that I can't afford to buy replacements and I've been getting the sewing machine out and putting it in action. I have old ball gowns that I could alter, outsized velvet tents that I could work with, and I'd splashed out at Christmas on a new red dress with sequins but I'm not really sure if it works. When I bought it I thought it was my dream dress because I'd dropped a good few sizes and although I got it on a mail-order catalogue, it was still the most glamorous thing I'd worn in years, but now I'm not so sure. Maybe I'd look like mutton dressed as lamb, maybe red satin and sequins is extraordinarily tacky. I just don't know what to wear anymore, I haven't dressed in a 'normal' size for years and what does one wear for a ball, and what does one wear for a photo-shoot? I have absolutely no idea and no faith in my judgment when it comes to this end of things. I've finally figured out how to sweat it out in a gym—I've learned how to walk, but I've really no idea how to dress myself.

I didn't start losing weight for cosmetic reasons or because of a feeling that I was fat or ugly. In fact, although many people now don't believe me, I actually had a good self-image even when I was at my heaviest. Maybe I was in denial, but most of the time I felt damned good about myself. I kept my hair conditioned and the roots touched up. Natural blonde? My dad was blond as a young man, but that's as close as I get! Over the years I had spent a fortune on clothes. I had so many shoes that an alien intruder would have been baffled to learn humans only have two feet. I had invested plenty of time and money in make-up and how best to apply it. But I hated photographs and would shy away from the camera at any occasion, knowing that I never seemed to get a flattering snap. It was not a good way to feel about photos when I had a fairly good idea that lots of photography was now lying ahead of me as we pushed out publicity for the trip and the Foundation. It was something that was only now dawning on me and something that I had never considered when I offered to go climbing mountains for Hope.

Along with not liking myself in photos, I also disliked catching sight of my reflection unawares in mirrors or shiny windows. Once I saw a tired, old woman coming towards me in a supermarket and almost died when I realised I had failed to recognise myself! Worrying and yes, perhaps that means I was a little in denial. Clothes, then, were definitely an issue as my shape began to change. I wasn't sure what to wear and I certainly couldn't afford to keep replacing what I had. Ironically, as I began to look better, I also began to be more critical of how I looked. How strange is that?

On many occasions before my health demanded that I lose weight, I did make frequent, failed attempts at diets and potions to make it happen quickly— quickly, but not easily. Anyone who thinks yo-yo dieters are taking the easy option clearly hasn't attempted to beat themselves into starvation for weeks at a time. They haven't suffered the appalling disappointment of restricting their life for weeks on end, only to see their hard-won gains disappear the moment they start eating 'normally'. They haven't tried replacing the joy of food with chemically flavoured powders, to the point where stealing a leaf of lettuce from a fridge late at night is enough to make a person cry with shame. It's a damned awful place to be. I've tried the Grapefruit Diet, the Cabbage Soup Diet, the Orange and Egg Diet, which involved so much flatulence I couldn't share a room! I've tried the horrible powdered meal replacements and I've tried Atkins, which only resulted in my developing cravings for foods I'd never eaten much of before, like pasta and potatoes and bread.

People look at people who are overweight and I'm convinced they believe they're looking at lazy self-indulgent people who hate exercise and love food. They couldn't be further from the truth. If you give up cigarettes or alcohol or drugs, you put those substances aside and avoid them. The poor unfortunate who needs to cut back on food also needs to eat food to survive—so cannot ever avoid their vice. I know I've said it before, but instead of a love affair with food, I think heavier people often have a 'hate affair' with food. You go for hours, reluctant or unable to eat, and then give way to hunger pangs and overeat or make bad food choices, then hate the food you're eating because you resent the effect it's about to have on your body.

These days I sometimes joke that I ate my way to fitness because I now eat every four hours and sometimes even more frequently than that, depending on my level of activity for the day. I also adore food now and eat such a wide range of foods that would never have been on my plate before. I used to love fried chicken and steak and cheese and I still do, but I was tightly limited to those choices and took pleasure eating those things, while also thinking I was being wicked or wrong. Now I enjoy those foods on occasion, but I also adore the taste of fresh basil with tomatoes, or honey and mustard on green leaves, the combination of apple and walnuts, or the unusual tang of rosemary in a salad or the sweetness of mint with beans or peas. I can genuinely lash into a bowl of strawberries and enjoy it more than chocolate cake. I eat a whole range of shellfish and lots of things I never tried to eat before like hummus, basil, olives, soya, asparagus and a whole list of other exciting food and ingredients. I'm always on the search for new tastes and flavours. It's given me a whole world of new choices and a whole range of freedom to eat, instead of the closed, hard, harsh environment of dieting and starvation. I love to eat. My WeightWatchers leader once commented in class that 'if you're hungry, you're going to eat—so there's no point being hungry'. Another of those simple statements that are so clear and obvious when you hear someone else mention them, but sometimes we need to hear the truth ring out loud before we hear it.

I suppose when I reached those very heavy weights, I failed to try and tackle the problem, partly because of the enormity of the challenge ahead. I genuinely thought it would take years to undo the damage I had done to myself. The thought of dieting for years and years just totally overwhelmed me and I was unable to face going on. It's not surprising; what mortal wouldn't feel daunted by the prospect of years of discipline stretching into the future? I also reckoned that my age was against me and there wouldn't be any point in being slim and attractive in my fifties because life would be over then. You may think that was incredibly stupid and defeatist, but it was simply my perspective, my point of view, the way I honestly felt. I was looking over a wall to the field beyond, but the wall was too high and I couldn't see the grass—so I didn't know it was greener out there! I also worried about my skin, I thought that even if I lost all my excess weight, I'd still be left with revolting, sagging skin and floppy boobs, and I couldn't see myself having surgery. I was condemning myself to misery and failure before I even began, so no wonder I kept failing.

I suppose the difference for me was my motivation. When the doctor told me that my health was not only in danger but was already affected, that my weight was preventing me from life-saving surgery, all the cosmetic reasons for dieting and the counter-arguments that went with them went out the window. The way I looked at it was radically changed, my perspective was altered, I could see over the wall and I knew I was going to climb over it, no matter how long it took. If the doctor had said, 'You have cancer,' my options would have been even further limited; if the doctor had told me I had heart damage, which was highly likely with my weight and my family's health history, again my options might have been limited. But the doctor was telling me there was life-saving surgery available to me—if I lost weight. The debate was over before it began. I stopped thinking about how long it would take to lose weight and started concentrating on simply making a difference. I still think that way today. I'm still battling to get to my goal weight and I still have a stone to go. I'm determined to get there, but I never think of the full amount, I just take it at a pound a time. Everyone can lose one pound. I just managed to keep repeating it and everyone can do that too.

Now that I was focused on 'getting healthy' instead of 'being beautiful' my age and the condition of my skin became less important to me. Ironically, both have become things that I'm proud of. I'm proud to say that I'm 45 and can run up eight flights of stairs. I'm proud, too, of my skin. It's not perfect, but I know what it's been through and it tells the story of where I've been, where I've come to and where I'm heading to. I don't need surgery either. When I visited my friend Google to search for what happens to skin when people lose weight dramatically, I read report after report saying that massive expanses of loose skin were unavoidable for someone undergoing the sort of weight loss that I've experienced. But they were wrong. I don't know if I'm just lucky with genetics or whether it was because I exercised so much, or because I drank and drink so much water (between 2 and 3 litres each day). What I do know is that I didn't use any special 'tightening' creams, because they were too expensive and I was spending too much money on the gym and other sports and exercises and the equipment that I needed to get out on the hills to have more left over for cosmetics. I did use Bio-Oil when I could afford it, but otherwise I lashed on any cheap moisturiser I could find.

My skin isn't perfect, but there are no big loose folds of skin, and I'm happy to get my arms and legs out—although my skin is definitely a bit crepey around my neck, inner thighs and the underside of my arms, especially if I'm moving against gravity! My tummy is still a work in progress because my extra stone seems to have decided to hang on there, my chest definitely needs a good bra and someone who knows how to fit it—but I'm quite chuffed with my butt! I'm being so brutally and embarrassingly honest because I know what it feels like for anyone with my sort of journey ahead. These are the types of questions that I couldn't find answers for anywhere. I'm not boasting about the fact that I'm happy with my skin and not too unhappy with my body shape overall—I want people to know that it's possible to go through all that effort and like what you end up looking like on the other side. I didn't know that in advance, I could only hope—and I want to shout it out loud and clear, it is worth hoping. If you want any advice on how best to make it happen, I'd say love yourself and feel laughter when you can, drink water, eat healthily instead of meanly, and exercise—enjoy feeling the growing strength of your body and love every moment of living. I truly believe if you feel strong inside, the rest follows.

So with all that positive energy I'm feeling, why was I absolutely terrified about what to wear to the Hope Ball? I'm smiling as I write, because I know it's easy to preach passionately about what you believe is true—but it's a different challenge to follow that truth in person every day. It's the lion and the mouse again. Dressing for that ball was a torment; it seemed to highlight every insecurity that I'd felt over the past ten years and bottle them—delivering them corked and intense like an overcooked wine. Preparations for that ball featured in 'The Big Book of Hope'—my first ever attempt at writing about my own journey. The Hope Foundation asked me to document my story for them as part of an 'anthology of hope' to raise funds for street kids in Kolkata in the run-up to Christmas. I was happy to help and later delighted to find my story nestled among 40 other wonderful writers ranging from my childhood heroine Maeve Binchy to popular politicians, amazing people like Beirut hostage survivor Brian Keenan and leading businessmen such as Bill Cullen and my own boss, Denis O'Brien. My little story for Hope talks about my struggle to lose weight and my Everest Base Camp challenge for The Hope Foundation, and culminates in this struggle over what I would wear to the Hope Ball.

Eventually it boiled down to the week leading up to the ball and I had decided, finally, not to buy something new but to pick from what I had and what

I could alter. My mum was playing Solomon and we had a major dress-trying-on session before going to bed.

Excerpt: 'Tapping into Hope'—from *The Big Book of Hope*

It's June 2010. A year ago I couldn't walk but today I'm catching a train to Kerry to meet Pat Falvey and the rest of the Expedition of Hope. We'll be climbing mountains for the next few days, a tough training camp to judge our progress in preparation for later this year. What better way to test a new body than to go for a stroll to Base Camp Mount Everest—the highest point in the planet? As the tap tap of my climbing poles replace the tap tap of my stick, I'll think of the incredible challenges and privileges that my whirlwind journey has brought me as it crashed through so many peaks and valleys to the foothills of the Himalayas.

Trying on dresses for The Hope Foundation Ball last March, my 82-year-old mum laughed and giggled as we ran between bedrooms. I'd dropped so many dress sizes that I was giddy with excitement and Mum was grinning too, from ear to ear. Finally deciding, we hugged and parted before going back to our rooms. But moments later she was back: 'Is that it? You're sure we've tried them all?'

'Yes, Mum, that's the lot.'

'So the fashion show is over?' she said.

'Yep, Mum, the fashion show is over.'

'Well, it's got to be the red,' she said.

Laughing, I agreed.

We hugged and kissed again, said, 'Goodnight, God bless,' and went to sleep.

Hope won't drag or drive me up Everest. But it stops me from giving up and giving in. It opened the door and whispered in my ear, telling me I could walk through it; and walk I will. I'll never wear the red dress. Mum never woke up. But when the time is right, I'll wear red again and remember her with love and laughter. And her strength and her spirit and her endless supply of hope come with me to Everest. It's not just my challenge any more, it's Mum's too. And everyone's who needs a bit of Hope.

Chapter 6
The Ladder to Everest

I was determined to make it to Everest Base Camp and now I had another reason to succeed. It would be my tribute to Mum. I never hesitated when I considered what to do and whether to give up the challenge and pull out of the expedition—I knew my mum would be furious if I'd done that and it would not have been something that she or I would be proud of. I would be using Mum's death as an excuse to opt out of something that was tougher than anything I'd ever done before. So the path was clear: my job was to push ahead ever harder than before and make sure that I not only succeeded, but succeeded well. The measure of my success would be the measure of my respect for my mum and my own personal pilgrimage. Maybe it is valuable when mourning to re-focus the mind elsewhere, to delay grief for all too short a time.

Maybe it's a coping mechanism to set a target, anything to deflect your heart from the crushing pain of reality that someone you loved and fought with, but always knew was on your team, was now outside your reach. I couldn't bring myself to linger much on that reality and didn't try to; I automatically shut down my emotions and mentally put them away in a box as I turned towards the struggle in hand.

The morning of my mum's funeral I went to the gym. I didn't admit that to many people, because I didn't think they'd understand, but I called my gym guru David and asked him to train with me and not to speak to me, but just train hard. We worked out and I poured every ounce of physical strength into the next hour. It was my way of saying sorry to Mum and releasing some of the feelings that I had pent up inside. Even planning the funeral details and getting panicked by the need to get everything right, the words of my Tipperary mountain leader came back to me and it was as if Mum was speaking the words too: 'Climb your own mountain, do it as best you see fit, do it your way, one step at a time, one foot in front of the other, it will all work out.' Later the feeling that I had paid a personal tribute to her in sweat and toil helped me get through the funeral, the speeches and the wake. We asked Mum's friends and relations to join with us in trying to remember her, not with sadness, but with love and laughter; and that's what I've tried to do since.

My Facebook page was now dramatically different to what it had been six months previously. It was littered with photos of training shots and beautiful images from the mountains and particularly my beloved Spink Mountain in Wicklow. As you know, I was now visiting Spink several times a week. On weekends I would get up at 6 a.m. and hit the mountain for 8, swinging up through the Miners' Village and around the saddle and back to the car park for a quick lunch, before changing direction and going up and around in the opposite direction from the steps, which is generally accepted as the toughest way of hiking the route. Because of the longer evenings, I was also able to head to the mountains after work. I did an early shift which allowed me to finish at 3 p.m. and be on the mountain by 4 and back down before 7. I generally managed to squeeze in one evening climb during the week along with the extra double push at weekends. Every morning was different, every evening was different, so many sights and sounds and different colours of light. One evening I came over the boardwalk under the brow of the summit and came across a herd of up to eighty or ninety deer grazing fearlessly, swept out across the boggy grassland that tumbled away to the cliffs that dropped down to the lake. They barely paid me any attention as I trotted past them on my way, but I gazed at them in delight.

Another evening, close to the end of my hike, as the light was fading a young man shouted out my name as I passed by. He was standing with a group of trekkers, taking a break near a bridge over a fast-flowing gully at the Miners' Village. At first I didn't stop, because my brain was reassuring me that no one I knew would be standing casually on a mountain as I passed by and he couldn't possibly be calling to me. Then a moment later I realised that he was, and I pulled up to chat, somewhat bemused. It turns out it was a young man called Ian Taylor, who in 2008 had become the youngest Irishman to stand on the top of the world and who was now running a budding new adventure company. He was also a friend of mine on Facebook and recognised me from the pictures of Glendalough training that I had posted online. We chatted about my plans to go to Everest Base Camp and what training I'd been doing and how much weight I'd lost and he was really positive about the Hope Expedition and my chances of success. I walked along the boardwalk with his group for a while and picked his brain about another element of the trip which I hadn't paid much attention to up to now. There was an extension to the expedition being planned, which some of the stronger members of the team were undertaking, to try and complete a technical summit on a peak in the Everest range called Island Peak. It stands 20,305 ft high and the climb involves crossing a glacier and dragging up an ice-wall with ice-picks and crampons, which are spikes that attach to your boots and adjust tightly to grip the ice while you're walking. If the gradient is steep enough, you may have to dig into the wall with your toes. Ian knew Island Peak very well and spoke with obvious pleasure and passion about its icy challenge. It sounded fascinating, but I was glad I wouldn't have to take on that level of difficulty. Only the super-fit members of the team would be attempting it and even then they had to pass a special fitness session with Pat Falvey later in the year, before he called the final cut on who would make the ascent.

I took advantage of this chance meeting with Ian and some of his climbing buddies, asking them all about trekking at altitude, about the difficulties of getting to Base Camp, of the traditions and culture, about what the food would be like and how to get water; lots of things that I had wondered about, but hadn't been able to find online, or didn't have access to experts to ask. He and his mates were great. They were enthusiastic and encouraging, with lots of information and helpful tips. They didn't make me feel stupid or daft for sweating my way around a mountain at 16 stone, while looking tentatively to the lofty heights of Mount Everest looming in just a few months' time. Not once did they look at me oddly or pass a glance of disbelief; they admitted to a certain level of surprise at the fact that I was having a go, but there wasn't so much as a whisper of cynicism and they clearly, genuinely wished me well. It was responses like this that fuelled my energy in the dark moments when my breath caught in my throat and I weakened and thought that perhaps I couldn't do it, or, more importantly, couldn't do it in time. I had so much catching up to do, my health and my muscles were so abused and they needed time they just didn't have to recover and grow and gain strength. It was constant, the feeling that a clock was ticking and I was in a race against myself, the mountain, and the very planet itself.

It was time to leave Spink for a while and head back to Kerry, this time with the whole Everest/Hope Expedition team. I was finally going to meet the rest of the celebrity gang and I was both excited and a little nervous. I'd spent several months getting fit and was now pushing my way around the Wicklow hills pretty effectively, but remember I'd started from a place of being 23 stone with a walking stick and a limp. I had a really long road to travel and I was nowhere near as fit as the rest of the team, who were healthy and sporty and had the added benefit of the fitness of youth. Our first meeting should have been at the Hope Ball, but of course I missed that because of my mum's passing, so now I had the added concern of being the last one in as well as the odd one out. We were going to have our first chance of bonding on the way down to Kerry, travelling by train courtesy of Irish Rail.

It was Friday; I finished work, parked the car securely in the 98fm car park and headed across town by taxi to catch the last train to Tralee. Bundling into Heuston Station with its beautiful but usually unnoticed architecture, I felt the familiar flush of excitement of arriving at a port for travel, be it by rail, air or sea. I looked across the vaulted halls and spotted Rosaleen. Both of us grinned like kids and I swear we both jumped up and down with excitement. There was garbled conversation and squeals of excitement as more team members arrived, Jenny Kavanagh of 'Fair City', RTÉ's Rob Ross and Ed O'Donnell, our technical support expert—who was later to acquire the name Dr Ed, because of his knowledge and belief in homeopathic remedies, as well as his comforting, kindly and reassuring air. We all hugged and kissed and I instantly knew these were good people. We chatted and giggled the whole way down to Tralee and bundled out of the train in a noisy explosion of hiking boots, rucksacks and walking poles, heading for the hills and this man Falvey, who we all had read about and watched on TV for years. The man himself rolled up in a silver Merc, greeting us warmly before introducing us to our minibus! Battle stations drawn—off we headed to Beaufort and Pat's Mountain Lodge. Of course I'd been here before, having made my earlier pilgrimage to Carrauntoohil. I was looking forward to getting back on the mountain and for a short time at least I even felt I had a slight advantage on the group, although of course I knew that wouldn't last.

The Hope/Everest team was growing again. Parking outside the Lodge, we met artist Philip Gray pulling up in his Porsche after driving up from Cork to join us. We met some of Pat's own World Wide Adventure Team, mountaineer Tony Nation and his wife Mary, and mountaineer, cameraman and computer and communications whizz Niall Foley. We were also joined by two more Hope recruits, Dave Walshe, a businessman and friend of the Foundation's from Cork who had been on walking trips to the Himalayas but was new to mountaineering, and Vivian Harrison, Hope's US Ambassador, stunningly pretty and later to become a lasting friend. George McMahon tumbled in. We'd later grow to accept that the gorgeous and adorable wee George would always turn up slightly late or not at all, in a charming state of chaos—except when it came to getting to the top of a mountain. There was loud chatter, wide smiles and a great sense of excitement in the air. It was dark now and Pat brought us into the warm, orange light of the Lodge and showed us around, street shoes tapping on wooden floors as we gazed at all the memorabilia and heard the stories about Everest and the Seven Summits, and Carrauntoohil, and native tribes in Papua New Guinea where Pat had lived for a time as part of his research into indigenous cultures under threat from the developed world. The night pushed on and Pat showed the team around the rest of the house, including his polar bear skin stretched out across his bedroom floor, a gift from an Inuit tribe in Canada where he had stopped off on one of his training sessions in preparation for a later expedition to the North Pole. He showed us the rest of the bedrooms, with their comfortable sleeping arrangements; soft, fluffy duvets and en-suite bathrooms with power shower . . . and finally, with a jarring, unexpected shift in direction, he showed us the door! As we viewed the tents and Portaloo set up in the back garden, I was sure I caught a devilish glint in Pat's eye. Softly spoken, he explained that he'd helped us out by setting up the flimsy canvas shelters for us, because we were so late down it would have been tough for us to have to do it ourselves. Our training for Everest had begun.

Quietened slightly, the group clambered into our 'tour bus' and headed off for dinner at Kate Kearney's Cottage in the Gap of Dunloe, counting our blessings that we were being fed in a restaurant and not having to make do with a bowl of Sherpa-style soup in the mess-tent. Kate's was buzzing with American tourists, traditional music and great Irish dancing—we even joined in and sang a few songs, passing around a pint glass to make a collection for our Everest Challenge and happily telling all who would listen about the mission that had brought us down to Killarney. We 'had the one' with dinner, highly conscious that we had a hard day ahead, an early start, and Ireland's highest mountain was standing by, ready to challenge us and punish the faint-hearted.

I woke in my tent to the sound of Jenny giggling. 'Jesus girl, you could snore for Ireland!' I groaned and rolled over, stretching and pleased that my tent buddy was giving me the bad news with a grin on her face. I love this girl. I was 16 stone and trust me, that really affects your breathing when you're asleep and doesn't make for happy bedfellows. 'Sorry. Was it that bad?' I asked. A chorus of yells from nearby tents answered me and I buried deep into my sleeping bag, cringing and calling out, 'Sorry, sorry, sorry' . . . laughingly mortified. Was it a good morning for climbing or was it just the orange fabric of the canvas flysheet filtering that warm glow on the light hitting down inside the tent? I emerged from my bag, gave Jenny a hug and reached for the zipper to open up a brand new day.

My heart caught in my smile as I perched on all fours and looked out across the sweeping valley and the lakes of Killarney shining in the early morning sun. Stepping forward and swinging my leg out over the lip of the tent, my foot pressed down on the cool, dewy grass, and I clenched my toes to feel the freshness of it. I reached behind me and tugged at the bedroll, dragging it out after me—an impromptu yoga mat. I stood up and walked across the grass, my toes damp and cool, bathed in the newness of Pat's green lawn. In the corner of the garden, slightly removed from the little gaggle of tents and overlooking yellow gorse and a standing stone, I threw down my mat at the foot of the lakes with the mountain behind me and began my yoga Sun Salute to the day, running easily through the flowing sequence, realising in a way I had never done before how the movements married with the earth and celebrated life and the joy of being alive.

Rejoining my new buddies in the mess tent, we whooped and laughed and salivated as Mary Nation and Pat's housekeeper Chris Doona brought out plates of bacon and sausage and egg: a real Irish breakfast to set us up for Carrauntoohil and the team's formal introduction to the highest mountain in Ireland. Boots and walking poles sorted, we clattered into the bus and were on our way to Cronin's Yard and the start of the day's hike. I felt no fear this time as we swung in from Cronin's to the stony track to the river bridge that took so many years to build. Stopping for the first photos of the day, I was reminded that we were now a part of an expedition that would be recorded for the media every step of the way. It was no longer a private experience because from here on, our training was being filmed at every turn and would be an archive file for the future. It didn't concern me, I'm used to living in the media eye, but I wasn't looking forward to the interviews that came with the job! I'm used to interviewing others and I had already found the experience of being interviewed myself quite strange. You could say the tables had turned and the watcher was now the watched.

Stepping out with the group, I quickly found my position . . . at the back. No surprise, I had no false expectations. Despite the months that I'd been training and walking and working out, I knew I still had a long way to go in catching up with the team in terms of strength and fitness. But I had no fear at this point, because I knew I had made it to the summit before and I knew if I had done it once, I could do it again. The pace was fast, I was comfortably warm, but I concentrated on relaxing and breathing and reminded myself of the mantra 'one step in front of the other'. With the speed of change that I was learning was typical for Carrauntoohil, the day had become murky and a light shower of rain hit us just as we approached the wall where I'd experienced my first 'scramble' just weeks earlier. I stepped back to allow for reactions from the rest of the team, excited also by their first engagement with the dark, craggy, sandstone. Rob and George hoofed up the 'Step of the Goat' in a couple of confident bounds; Ed and Philip also had no problem, strong and steady. I was in my element of course, having loved it first time round and thrilled to be swinging off it again. Rosaleen and Vivian tackled it with a stern frown of concentration and possibly a less than polite phrase hovered beneath Viv's lip, but we all made it up and over with grins at the top and no major events.

We traversed across the foot of the mountain towards Cummeenoughter Lake, the highest lake in

Ireland with the minerals in the ground adding to its mystic, brilliant blue, and on towards a number of the gullies heading for the top, but suddenly I was shaken out of my comfort zone as I realised we'd taken a different route. I hadn't been this way before and mentally I'd lost my advantage. My first trip out on Carrauntoohil we swept around Cummeenoughter and headed up loose scree, a broad ascent to the summit along Brother O'Shea's Gully; but now I was sure I was looking at the lake from a different angle. I'd jump-started my way into hiking, learning none of the traditional skills along the way. Caught up in my race to the top, I had lost out on the basic skills of navigation and mapping, I couldn't read a compass and I couldn't figure out where I was; my head was swimming and I was totally lost. I wasn't afraid, because I was with the group and following them, but I became intensely aware for the first time that I was walking across a mountain with absolutely no knowledge of where I was or what I was doing. Later, looking back, I find it strange that the thought didn't hit me on my first trip out. I think I was then so focused on my fitness and the need to simply keep walking that I didn't have the luxury of expanding my thoughts further than that. This time I was stunned that having walked the mountain once, I didn't recognise the points around me.

It was a lesson for the future on how easy it is to take a mountain for granted and how changing conditions can create chaos in an instant for the ill-prepared or those who don't respect the hills around them and their ability to muddle and confuse careless climbers. Ironically, the fact that I was aware I was in unfamiliar terrain showed that I was learning to become aware of my surroundings, but at the time I didn't see that as a positive. My breathing got raspy as my confidence slipped and I slowed right down. The mist turned into a dirty rain and I found I was wet through my waterproofs, bathed in sweat on the inside while the rain streamed down from the peak on my hood, making me feel like a damned duck. I was awkward, hot, steamy, uncomfortable, unsure and unhappy. I plodded along. I was conscious that I was among the slowest of the group and it did nothing to boost my confidence as we approached what I now know to be Curved Gully.

I looked with disbelief as I saw Pat and Niall heading for what appeared to be a waterfall heading down the side of Carrauntoohil. Surely they can't possibly mean for us to head up there? In horror the dawning realisation deepened that this was, in fact, the plan. I looked at the excited faces around me and wondered was I the only one who thought this was complete lunacy. At the height of my cowardice I looked towards Vivian and Rosaleen, who were shaken by the scramble at the 'Step of the Goat', thinking surely they would save me by making a fuss and then we could all retreat to sanity and safer ground. To my astonishment Rosaleen looked unperturbed and Viv a little nonplussed but not digging her heels in at all. I had to admit, it seemed it was just me who was absolutely appalled at the thought of clambering up this steep, slippery waterfall with its jagged rocks, bound to be covered in slime from the flowing water and bound to be treacherous, as all the while the rain continued to beat down on top of us. Philip Gray piped up, 'I did this once before, great fun, this is great.'

Listening to him, my heart sank. What had I let myself in for? 'This is the type of madness that people who climb mountains enjoy, for them this is what it's about, these people are all going to Base Camp Mount Everest and I'm a clown who tagged along for the ride and found herself totally out of her depth, I must have been crazy to get involved or think that I could do something this extreme. It's good enough losing weight, I don't have to lose my life. Nuts, these people are nuts—and I'm insane to be going along for the ride. The charity? Okay, I'm committed, but I'm not too far down the line; I can bail, do something else—stand with a bucket on O'Connell Bridge for the rest of the summer if needs be, I don't have to do this.'

Pat's voice cut across my increasingly frantic, angry thoughts. 'You alright for this?' he said. 'I don't know,' I answered honestly, without hesitating to analyse the response. 'Well, we better find out,' and he was gone. Up, bounding from rock to rock and disappearing into the cascading gully. As he disappeared from view, my one comforting thought was the sight of the rope coiled heavily over his shoulder. At least if I got stuck on this damned watery stairway, there would be some hope of pulling me out of it or letting me down.

There's a skill for climbing a narrow gully like this. You learn to 'bridge', to step on footholds on either side of the gully and form a human bridge with your body that arches away from the centre. There are two advantages; it allows you to stay far enough away from the rock to be able to spot where to put your feet, allowing you to pinpoint clear footholds rather than slithering around trying to gain purchase on loose water-covered scree. It also keeps you out of contact with the cascade of water flowing down towards you. It works very well and makes short work of what would otherwise be a messy, wet scramble. I had none of those skills. I instinctively clung to that gully like a limpet, wedging my 16 stone deep into the crack, feet shoved in as far forward as I could get them, my still-substantial belly shoving my shoulders back out towards the empty space behind me. I was like a beached whale, half in and half out on the shore, sweating, breathing harsh with exertion and panic. I was totally unbalanced and totally soaked by the waterfall lashing down on top of me. If I'd brought a diving snorkel to breathe through, it wouldn't have looked out of place. I was absolutely petrified, I was angry, cold and wet, shivering with all of the above and cursing Pat Falvey with every cell of my being. I kept moving my feet up, inch by inch, clawing for new grips with my hands, which were scratched and bleeding. I couldn't have given up if I had wanted to; there were a string of climbers behind me in the gully and Pat and his rope were a million miles up ahead. Plodding along, one foot in front of the other, I kept going and Rob Ross was my saviour. 'Shall I give you a shove?' he politely and rather humorously inquired. 'Yes please,' I responded as I stalled yet again, hunting for another inch of height. 'Well if you don't mind me pawing your bum,' he said. 'Haul ass away,' was my laughing response—truly, I was beyond embarrassment and Rob continued to push me up that gully to the top. On our first training trip to Kerry Rob Ross climbed my mountain as well as his own!

It was a tough struggle but we all made it to the top of that section of the gully, then crossed out and traversed along a less steeply ascending scramble to the top and onwards to reach the cross at the top of Carrauntoohil, battle scarred but never weary. The cross was charred and blackened from lightning strikes but just like the first time I saw it, it called to me through the mist and welcomed me home. We took a breather at the top, drank water, ate our sandwiches and feasted on Dr Ed's seemingly inexhaustible supply of chocolate and treats which was to become legendary for the course of the entire Everest expedition. Finally we turned around and headed over the edge to begin our descent down the much eroded Devil's Ladder with warnings from the guides about loose scree and slipping and knocking and the danger of pushing rocks down on climbers below. We carefully picked our way down; still focused but all clearly relieved that the day was nearing an end and we had the summit under our belts, with sore feet and blisters and shoulders and legs screaming. We stopped briefly for coffee at Cronin's Yard before boarding the bus and heading back to the relative comfort of our tents and Portaloo on Pat's garden lawn.

A change of clothes later we were good to go and went off to Kate Kearney's Cottage for a hot meal and another night's entertainment. Pat took off the brake, we had drinks and craic and even joined the dancers, despite our sore joints. He allowed us to pick the time for our return back to the tents. Some left a little early. I joined the naughty crew and stayed a little later, finally taking a tired body but a happy soul back to the Lodge around 11 p.m. We tumbled into our sleeping bags amid another round of laughter and giggles with Pat calling down mock flatteries from his comfy perch inside the Lodge, from his bedroom under the eaves. He leant out through a window which looked out over the lawn and our tent-village, calling out and joining in the giggled jokes as we all settled in for the night. 'Good night,' he finally called, and we all rolled over and drifted off to sleep. About three hours later, the alarm went off.

The descriptive nouns I designed for that man have no place on the page. Groans echoed around the tents as we realised we were being pulled out of our relatively warm bolt-holes to stick on damp gear and go back out on a mountain. Among the least impressed was our young spitfire Jenny, who let Pat have it verbally with two barrels, to his obvious amusement. Our ranting was in all honesty accompanied by a frisson of excitement and also the tiniest, slightest thrill at being caught out and challenged. I felt a bit like a kid again, when someone else was calling the shots and everything was new and surprising. We tumbled into the mess tent to find a laughing Tony Nation boiling kettles and Niall the cameraman adjusting lights. 'Get that thing away from me,' growled Jenny, but we were all learning that the sparkle in her eye belied her attempts at being grumpy. The actress was playing a role and charmingly so. I love that girl to death. All the personalities of the group were manifesting themselves under the unusual conditions of the weekend and, delightfully, we all slotted wonderfully into place. The joker, the clown, the grump, the medic, the artist, the writer, the comedian, the therapist, the counsellor—all the bases were covered and we already knew we had a good team that would pull together well. There were no loose links and we all contributed something to the mix. I had clean clothes and dry socks but sitting in the mess tent we all began to realise that our outer clothes, our waterproofs and our boots were soaking. That hurt even more than the lack of sleep and the early hour. We ate a somewhat muted breakfast, loaded up with fresh water and supplies of chocolate and donned wet boots to follow Pat and his guides back into the hills.

We were back in the bus heading out into the darkness and joking and laughing again, teasing and larking; adult juvenile delinquents on a day out from school. There was no sign of the big expedition chiefs, the wanderers, the explorers, the hardened adventurers who were planning on making it to Base Camp Mount Everest. We were a gang of naughty kids in damp boots heading off into the night for excitement. We bundled out of the bus by the side of a road somewhere in the dark, then started climbing. Pat, the Peter Pan of the Gap, stepped out and we followed across turfy, peaty ground. Our head torches casting a yellow glow across our faces, illuminating us eerily in the night, the musty smell of bog and bruised ferns permeating the air around us, the ground steepened and began to pull on tired legs. I pushed down hard on my walking poles, sucked in my gut and bent my head so that the lamp on my forehead pointed out dry rocks to step on amid the soft, spongy, muddy ground. It was hard going, but now I felt good. After the nervous exhaustion of the day before, I was back in my element. Hard slog I could handle, weeks of walking up my mountain in

Wicklow paid off, as I plodded along, one foot in front of the other. I wasn't the fastest in the group, I didn't expect to be, but I was steady and I wasn't suffering. I was confident and my legs and knees and back felt good as we pushed on ever higher.

The ground began to change and we left the soft, boggy peat behind and stepped onto stony ground. Even in the dark, the stones looked distinctive, jaggedly broken and uneven. It was sandstone and I later learned we were climbing Purple Mountain, which gets its name from the purple glow it sends out when seen from afar. The climb got tougher and steeper, the rocks unstable, moving beneath my feet. I was getting better at judging where to step, at connecting the balls of my feet with the rock and placing the balance of my weight squarely across my hips. No one told me this; it just seemed to happen as my body adjusted to the rough terrain. Poor Vivian was having a tough time, breathing laboured and making jerking, jagged movements as she walked. Pat suddenly stopped, calling out, 'Vivian, come up here beside me, I want you at the front.' There was a near-rebellion as Viv demurred, absolutely hating being the centre of attention and making it very clear that the last place she wanted to be in the world was walking beside Pat. 'I want you here,' he repeated and Viv, head hanging low, moved to the top of the line. It was a pattern that would later be repeated on Everest and Viv's reaction was always the same when the call rang out, 'Vivian, come up here beside me.' The rest of us would laugh. Poor Viv, but she's a survivor and would surprise us all later—and perhaps herself too.

It was tough and hard and incredibly special, as the mist of dawn swirled around my boots then started to rise up into the air and the sun sent pink and purple fingers across the top of the mountain, sweeping in towards us as we approached the summit. An unspoken energy coursed through us all as without comment or debate, we realised that we were likely to hit the top just as the sun rose. We pushed as one, picking up the pace and heading always upwards, a measured, fluid movement now in our stride, tired legs forgotten. As the summit approached, Tony Nation warned us we had further to go, explaining there were 'false' summits on Purple Mountain and we needed to make it through to the third and final peak. We made it. The group poured over the top of the mountain as the sun spilled over the edge of the world, purple, pink, bruised, with the promise of new hope, new dreams, new possibilities. We laughed and hugged and danced in the early morning light, mist banished, fears gone, pain forgotten. We realised for the first time this was now a team.

We headed back down the mountain to the Gap of Dunloe, stripping down to our underwear to plunge into an icy river pooled between the lakes, screaming as the bitter cold grabbed at sore feet and ankles and higher, catching our breath as the icy bands pressed around our chests, and then the rush of warm blood filled our veins and filled us with life and energy and fun. Roughly rubbing down, dressing and trundling off down the road back towards Kate's and the bus that was waiting there, and back to Pat's to debrief and review how far we'd come.

Back at Pat's we graduated from the tents and were allowed power showers and breakfast, before joining in high spirits in the lounge to discuss our progress, thrilled with ourselves and delighted at what we'd achieved. 'You're too slow,' Pat shocked us down to earth. Stunned, we looked around the room, every face registering disappointment and small measures of disbelief. 'You need to knock at least three hours off climbing Carrauntoohil before I'd even consider any of you doing Island Peak.' Base Camp? someone asked. 'It's doable,' Pat replied, 'but there's still a lot of work to be done.' He went on to explain about altitude and the need for mountain fitness. He pointed out that what we needed on a three-week expedition to Everest was endurance. It's not simply the ability to be super fit and to walk for eight hours at altitude with your legs and lungs screaming—but to be able to come back out the next day and do it again, and again, and again. I mentally thanked my little gym guru David, who'd said pretty much the same thing without ever climbing a mountain—he'd obviously done his homework and done his job; hopefully I'd do mine. 'Imagine this level of endurance for Base Camp,' Pat said, adding, 'For Island Peak, imagine having to go beyond that again. You'll be walking for days to reach Base Camp for Island Peak, then you'll have to push ahead up to rest at Middle Camp, then push up again to High Camp, before getting up in the middle of the night to scramble up solid rock for four hours before crossing a glacier, dragging up a fixed rope on an ice-wall to an icy ridge-walk to finally reach the summit.' Pat stressed the difficulty of walking with ice-picks and crampons; of walking roped together and the very real threat that one slip could put yourself and the rest of your team in danger. He explained the techniques that needed to be learned, such as ice-arrests, where you use your ice axe to stop a fall on ice and slow a slide that would otherwise pull you and your team down the glacier and into a crevasse, crashing into the abyss below.

The giddiness was completely banished as Pat slowed and looked solemnly around the room. The cameras were rolling on but forgotten in the corner and our faces were grim as he slowly asked us to tell him who was prepared to put the training in for Everest Base Camp and who would be aiming for Island Peak. As he swept his eye across the room, each member of the team reviewed their own progress, stated where they thought their fitness lay, how it could be improved and whether they were capable of aiming for Island Peak. The penetrating gaze spun around to me and I had no doubts. I calmly told Pat that I would love to go to Island Peak but I knew I didn't have the techniques it required and didn't believe I had the time to acquire them. 'I think hard work can get me to Base Camp,' I said. 'I believe Base Camp is a realistic goal and I'm determined to focus on getting there. But I'm not quick enough or fit enough to tackle Island Peak and I don't want to put the team in danger by being the weak link. I'll do Base Camp.' Pat thanked me for my honesty and moved on.

There had never been any question of me taking on the extension to the challenge and going for Island Peak. It was never an option, so why did I feel so empty walking out of Pat's lounge? I hung back as we were preparing for the train back to Dublin and asked for a quick word with the man himself. 'You've seen me on the mountain and you've seen the progress I've made, but you've also seen how slow I am and how much work I still have to do to get fit,' I said. 'Have I made the right decision? I feel I'm being responsible about opting out of Island Peak, but I still feel a part of me would like to have a bash. Could I do it?'

Pat was kind, telling me how well I'd already done, how he was astonished to see how I kept up with the group over the course of the weekend, how my fitness had improved dramatically since my last trip to Kerry and how he knew the effort and hard work that must have gone into that. But he also pointed out that Island Peak was a whole different ball game, involving rope techniques and harnessing and climbing skills that I'd never experienced. Base Camp would still be challenge enough, he said, but he went on to say that he thought at this stage that I would make it there.

'But Island Peak,' I pressed.

'You don't have the speed,' Pat replied. 'What am I lacking?' I pressed again. 'You don't have the fitness, you don't have the strength and you don't have the technical knowledge.' I thanked him for his honesty and the wonderful weekend, and headed for the train.

Chapter 7
Wheels and Walls

I knew I couldn't do Island Peak. I knew I'd made the right decision in opting out. After all it wasn't as if I had ever opted in. I hadn't been asked to go to Island Peak, I'd been asked to go to Base Camp, and that was what I was training for. As it was, I would be hugely impressed with myself if I got that far. It's an extraordinary challenge for any mortal to tackle altitude and days of walking uphill without picking up an injury or just packing in. I mustn't demean that effort for an instant or start feeling demotivated because others were doing something more challenging than me. I knew I was coming from behind in the fitness stakes, and I knew it was silly to imagine that I could run ahead with the twenty-somethings and pretend that I was as fit and lean as them. I was still hauling several stone of extra bulk along with me and the climb up Curved Gully should have shown me how incredibly far behind I was with the rest of the group. I had to be realistic, be practical about what I could achieve, aim for it—and go and get it. There was also the element of danger. I could run off on a mad challenge and end up making other people responsible for me and possibly endanger them in the process. It would be hard enough for them to get to Base Camp, not to mention pushing ahead for Island Peak, but they certainly wouldn't need to be balancing themselves on a rope and towing me behind them. No, I'd made the right decision. What did Pat say about the technical aspect too? I didn't know how to tie on a harness, or tie a proper knot. I didn't know how to tie in to a rope or how to abseil, any of those things. Of course when I thought about it, those things I could learn without being fit. That's just knowledge. 'He's right,' I thought. It's pure ignorance to go to the highest mountain in the world and then start learning stuff like that, if you're not prepared to learn how to do it on your own mountains first. It somehow seemed disrespectful not to afford the mountain the courtesy of being prepared. Somewhere close to the outskirts of Dublin on the way up from Kerry, I suddenly realised that I could at least do that.

I set off for Trinity College Dublin later that week. Rosaleen, my Hope Foundation leader and already now my friend, came with me. I had rung up the college, explained we were heading off to Everest on a charitable mission and asked if they could help us out with some time on their climbing wall. They were absolutely brilliant and set aside 40 hours of access to the wall and their instructor, Jonathan Fitzpatrick. I was nervous and excited arriving at TCD and heading to the sports complex for the first time. Their climbing wall faces out onto a busy Dublin street, across from Pearse Street train station, and I had often walked past and looked up to see nimble young tearaways dancing up the coloured pins on the wall, thinking how cool and athletic they looked but never for a moment thinking that it was something I could—or would want to—try. Now I was here, tying on a pair of loaned climbing shoes that were pinching hell out of my toes, and wondering, not for the first time this year, what on earth I'd got myself into. Jonathan was wonderful, very calm and confident with a dry humour running pleasantly through his personality. There was no hint that he thought we were ridiculous, two gals in their forties turning up on his doorstep to step awkwardly into a harness and start learning about knots and ropes for the first time. He had a lovely laid back fair-play attitude that made me feel totally open about trying anything and having a go. He helped me step into the harness, a bulky, confusing tangle of straps that took me a while to figure out, and he explained about double looping the main strap back through the buckle for protection.

Content that we were tightly strapped in, Jonathan then showed us both how to tie a 'figure of eight' knot. Both Rosaleen and I were good students, giggling a bit, but still focusing enough to get the hang of it pretty quickly. Jonathan later gave me a stretch of rope to take home and practise knots on. I would have felt silly telling anyone, but each night I'd turn the light off and spend a little time practising my 'figure of eight' in the dark. I thought I'd try and be fool-proof so that nerves wouldn't eat away my knowledge if I ever needed to use the knot in an emergency on a mountain.

Next was a lesson on how to belay, which is what you call the technique used by one climber to rope-support another climber on the wall. The buddy who stands below runs the rope through a small metal clip, a 'bug' or belay device, which takes the pressure off and works as a lever to give you more control. Safely tying on to the rope, the bug and the harness are vital for the climber's safety. Jonathan calmly explained that the actual harness and attachments are easy and quick to set up, but absolutely essential, and he drove home the importance of checks and double checks before the climber starts to ascend. We got it and finally, I got my chance to do it. Safely harnessed and roped, I moved closer to the wall and looked at the coloured pins in front of me, the idea being to pick a colour and follow the route of those pins up the wall. 'Climber ready?' asked Jonathan. 'Climbing on,' I replied, following the drill with a nervous grin, and I reached for the first red pin. My feet were squeezed into tiny little climbing shoes that had a rubber sole which clearly gave good traction on the wall, but they hurt. As I reached my left foot up to the first red pin, I hooked my toe over the top and pressed down on the ball of my foot. Stepping up, I naturally switched my body's weight onto my left foot, swinging my hip to the left and bringing my right toe up a little further up the wall to find another tiny red pin and press down again, reaching simultaneously higher with my left hand, then the right, then pulling up, identifying the next foothold and repeating the process, higher again. My poor head for heights didn't give me any trouble; I was too busy concentrating on the wall in front and the pins above to even think about looking down.

As I moved higher up the wall, I felt a rhythm developing with the movement of my body, swinging hips, redistributing weight, stretching arms and legs and testing and pulling muscles and limbs. It felt good, it felt like dancing, almost like yoga. I felt I was using my body in a way I'd never thought of using it before and I was astounded and delighted at its flexibility and strength. It was like I was outside looking in and liking what I saw. I wasn't arrogantly admiring myself, but I was appreciating what this battered, bruised body was achieving after all I'd put it through and after all those years of pain and stiffness of not being able to climb the stairs, my God, here I was dancing up a wall at a young person's university in the middle of Dublin City. How many times I'd dreamed of just being able to walk without pain and look at me now. My eyes filled with tears, but I kept them there and laughed instead. Reaching the top I triumphantly whooped and cried out, terribly uncool, but who cared? Jonathan and Rosaleen laughed with me as I pushed away from the wall and bounced down, pushing my feet against it with bent knees as instructed. My first abseil. Life was never so good. We climbed for over an hour and I knew that, technical knowledge aside, this was something I wanted to do again and again.

I had another challenge looming now, something I wasn't quite sure how to handle. I'd never fundraised before, but I wanted to raise €6,000 for this trip, as the whole point of the expedition was to raise cash for a girls' home for The Hope Foundation's base in Kolkata. Hope gives support and education to street kids there, aiming to break the cycle of poverty and help young people to help future generations. They even run a hospital. It's an amazing project and I was enormously proud to be involved. In the past, I'd always been happy to throw a few bob in a pot or buy a line for someone running a race or swimming for charity, but I'd never sat down with a plan to raise a set amount of money. As a journalist I am only too aware of the world's problems and the extent of the difficulties so many people face. I think I've always lived in a certain amount of denial about it, reporting the troubles around me but never attempting to fix them, simply because of the size of the mountain to climb. I always thought that whatever small thing I could do would just be a drop in the ocean and totally pointless. I mentioned this once to Rosaleen. 'Do you know what hope stands for?' she asked, smiling at me. I shook my head. 'Hope stands for "Help One Person Everyday",' she smiled. It was one of those Eureka moments, like when the dietician asked me what was in my fridge. I thought about all the days of my life when I could have helped one person—and didn't. If I had helped one person every day for thirty or forty years, how many would I have helped? That would have been a lot more than a drop in an ocean. I would have really made a difference. Well, I couldn't help by looking backwards, but I could certainly make a difference going forwards. The thought put a completely different perspective on the challenge of fundraising. Before I was nervous and overwhelmed by the enormity of what I had to do; now I was concentrating, not on me, but on the kids. I could make a difference.

As Head of News at 98FM, I'm used to organising, building protocols and pressing through to achieve results. I'm used to dealing with the media, I'm used to instructing teams, acquiring assets and resources, researching, interviewing, making headlines, speaking to people, communicating with individuals and organisations, keeping records and inventories, being creative and adding a healthy dose of reality to take good ideas and make them work. I probably didn't realise I had these skills until I started organising my fundraising and then I found I needed every single one and more! Thankfully I made a couple of good choices at the start, which was more to do with luck than skill. I instinctively decided to design my fundraising around people, places and things that were close to me and I think that made a huge difference because it made me feel passionate about the events I organised. It also gave me the comfort of being on home ground.

Because I love old cars I decided to organise something around classic cars and ask for help from my MX5 car club. I also love Slane Castle, which was the scene of my first rock concert during one summer a million years ago . . . Despite being struck by a severe dose of hero worship, I steeled myself and contacted Slane Castle to ask Lord Henry Mountcharles and his family if we could stage a car run from the Phoenix Park to his home and hold a picnic in the grounds. I then contacted the vintage and classic car clubs and issued an invitation to come along and take part in a contest for 'best picnic', 'best turned out car' and 'best turned out driver'. Everyone agreed to get on board and the 'Cars at the Castle' event was born. The Mountcharles family were stunning; not only did they agree to host the day but Lord Henry's son Alex agreed to lead the rally and turned up in the Park with a drop-dead gorgeous classic white E-type Jag to drive all the way back to Slane under Garda escort. It was great fun, and a huge success, but if I'd realised how ambitious I was being I would never have attempted it. Organising a car rally with classic cars involves the need for insurance, safety marshals, safety plans and tow-away services. It's tremendously difficult and complicated, but it all worked out brilliantly—partly because my own ignorance forced me into doing things one step at a time.

I thought I could use my own recent training experience for another event, so decided to do a 'treadmillathon'—walking for eight hours on my battered old treadmill at my local Superquinn. I got the word out on the radio in advance and my WeightWatchers girls gave me an enormous surprise by turning up on the day with a second treadmill, popping it beside me and taking turns throughout the day to walk along with me. They were great and I was incredibly touched, both with them and with my 85-year-old father, who insisted on standing on his feet to shake a tin beside me all day long. On the way home, he told me he was proud of me and I thought I would burst with pride myself. What a lovely man I'm blessed with having as my dad.

I mentioned to Rosaleen that we really needed a spectacular event. I felt we needed to do something controversial or quirky to get the public's attention, to attract some media interest and give us a chance to let people know what we were doing. Hope already had a website up and running and I also had a blog published on the 98FM website, but I worried that unless we pushed people to these pages, they could remain there undiscovered and pointless. Lots of ideas were dreamed up and discarded before Rosaleen turned to me idly with a crazy idea that she seemed to pluck out of mid-air. The whole team were together again, being fitted out for expedition clothes at Basecamp in Middle Abbey Street in Dublin, which was sponsoring our expedition gear. We'd been chatting and laughing with Jack, the owner, when Rosaleen suddenly caught my eye and blurted out, 'You could always abseil down the Wheel of Dublin.' Huh?

Jack started laughing with a glint in his eye. 'You could,' he helped her out.

'I couldn't,' I quickly fitted in. We went on looking at gear but after a while I mumbled, 'Pat might know how to do it.' Rosaleen was on to my moment of weakness like a light, ringing Pat on the spot. A few moments later I was speaking to the big man.

'You could do it alright,' he said, 'but you won't make any money and it will distract from your training. It would take months to organise.' I hung up, passed the phone to Rosaleen and with a large measure of relief pronounced that it wasn't a runner, too difficult, too complicated and much too late.

Later, in the car on the way home, I pulled in and gave my rescue buddies in the Coast Guard a call, a further call shortly afterwards to Mike O'Shea from 'Work at Height Training Ltd', one of the country's leading working at height and rescue training companies, and 10 minutes later a phone call back to Rosaleen: 'We're doing it!' I hung up on her screams, gunned the engine and with my heart racing, I drove home.

About a month later I was driving down the quays on a calm, rather misty morning. It was August and the early morning sun was shooting pink fingers across the skyline and you could feel the heat building, knowing the mist would burn off quickly as soon as the warmth of the morning spilled over the edge. I was calm, but catching my eyes in my rear-view mirror I could read a sense of doom in my expression. I wondered about my sanity. When I know I'm scared of heights, why on earth would I not only agree to abseil down the country's largest Ferris wheel, but actually push to make it happen?

I turned on the radio as I drove, but the dial was tuned to my own station, 98FM, and the Morning Crew breakfast show were excitedly 'talking it up' about their Head of News, who was about to leave the safe confines of the newsroom and throw herself down a rope from the top of the 197-ft-high Wheel of Dublin. They explained that it was for The Hope Foundation, and for the day they renamed the massive Ferris wheel Teena's Wheel of Hope. Sickened, I

switched the radio off and hit the CD. Home-town
rockers U2 filled the speakers and I groaned as I heard
the lyrics 'I will climb these city walls only to be with
you.' I burst out laughing. Okay, time to have one of
those conversations I have with myself: 'Give it a miss
and stop being a drama queen, stop the messing,
you're on a rope and Mike won't drop you, he doesn't
want the insurance claim!' I grinned again as I
continued the long drive down the quay with the big
wheel looming up in the foreground, silhouetted
against the mouth of the harbour as the Liffey rolls
lazily down into Dublin Bay.

Pulling up at the base, I waved to the crowd already
gathered there, winked at the cameramen—we're in
this together—and made my way over to Mike for
instruction. We had a schedule to keep. As well as
abseiling down the wheel, I needed to make links to
the radio station, who were running their morning
breakfast show around the drop, and I needed to
make live links back to my own newsroom, so there
was quite a bit of organising. We needed audio for the
radio before and after the drop and the snappers—or
photographers—had to be facilitated. I was doing this
for publicity and I've lived long enough behind a
microphone to know what these media teams needed
and how to make their lives easy. It felt strange to be
on the other side of the fence, but I suppose it gave
me an advantage. Smile, be pleasant, no dramas; give
them information and deal with them quickly—some

can stay and watch, others have headlines and need to grab a quick interview and run. Concentrating on the organising kept me too occupied to worry about nerves, until suddenly Mike took my arm, looked me in the eye and said, 'Right, you're mine now.' That was it, I was switching gear now, needed to concentrate and focus; no screaming, no hesitations, forget about the nerves and think about the process. I instinctively knew that panic and fumbling cause mistakes and accidents, so it was in my own best interest to get a grip and keep the nerves under control.

I was harnessed up and I was roped up and I jumped into the cab of the Ferris wheel with Mike and started rolling up to the top of the wheel. The view was stunning and Dublin looked magnificent in the early morning sun. I still had a sinking feeling in my stomach but I refused to acknowledge it, looking at the sun glancing off the River Liffey and the mouth of Dublin Bay. I looked at the city's skyline, which had altered stunningly in recent years, and I pushed aside wild thoughts to concentrate on the benefits I could clearly see from the Celtic Tiger economy. I gazed admiringly at the glassdomed front of Dublin's new Convention Centre that seemed to hang suspended over the river. I looked over at the architecturally unusual Grand Canal Theatre, another spectacular new addition. Up and down the river on both sides I could see the developments of recent years and realised that even though we'd been hit by recession, the city had an awful lot to be grateful for. It was truly beautiful up there; maybe I had a sense of euphoria born of pure panic, but I felt totally peaceful and incredibly happy with myself and the world. Mike's smooth movements with the ropes impressed me and gave me confidence. 'At least he looks like he knows what he's doing,' I thought, then switched the thought process because it wasn't taking me to pleasant places.

Finally, perched at the top of the world, Mike chucked my rope outside the cab, watching it tumble down to the ground below. He tested it and turned to me. There was a medley of ropes and knots hanging in arcs from the ceiling of the cab and Mike nodded to me to step out through them, not, it seemed, a man of many words. (I'd later find I was wrong about that.) I stood out to the edge of the cab and turned to face him, following his instructions. I leaned out, holding the open cab on the left and right, with my feet balanced on the ledge. I heard my name called from outside the cab and, surprised, glanced left and realised that I'd forgotten about the photojournalists who were strapped in in the cabs below on either side. I smiled and threw one hand loose to pose, then turned my face to repeat the process for the snapper on my other side. A few more shots and wide smiles and then Mike took control. 'Forget the photo-shoot,' he growled, and, looking me straight in the eye, he gave me the order to step off.

I stepped back into space and caught my breath as the rope took my weight. It gave a little, then held, and I remembered to breathe again, reminding myself that I had a safety rope tied to my harness and it was virtually impossible for me to fall. It was still a very long way up and I paused, hanging there for a moment before looking up at Mike, giving him an okay with my left hand, then releasing the brake rope that I had gripped tightly in my right. I held my brake-hand low down on my right thigh and I guided the rope through the belay as I began to lower myself 60 m (196 ft) to the ground below.

I'd had no idea how I would react when asked to step out of the cab but I'd beaten myself up all the way down the quays that morning. I knew the abseil would probably be over in five minutes, gone in a heartbeat, in an instant and in years to come, even if the Ferris wheel was removed, I wanted to drive past Dublin City Quay and remember the occasion, not the fear. I need not have worried. I loved it.

Abseiling on the wheel was different to abseiling on the climbing wall, which I'd tried for the first time just two days before. This time there was no firm structure to push or bounce off—the first 10 metres (30 ft or so) of the abseil was made directly into space, just dropping myself down on the end of the rope. When I came in line with the first struts of the wheel, I knew I had to push against them, to avoid getting caught up in the spines of the wheel and making a mess.

Having a task to do also stopped me worrying about the height and getting nervous. I calculated each strut, the push against it, and the swing it would generate, while dropping down to connect with the strut below. It was tricky enough and I was also giving a running commentary to a radio mike as I made the descent. I was amazed afterwards when I listened back to the tape, surprised that I had talked so much and so fluidly about the beauty of the city, the landscape, the cars below, the regeneration of the docklands and the gift of belief and hope and courage for the future. Adrenaline does funny things to a girl!

Finally I bounced down onto the platform below and kept bouncing, the give in the rope pulling me up and down with the momentum of the landing. I laughed with relief and delight at the roar of the crowd, the clapping and screams and hugs all around as microphones emerged under my mouth and the radio station hungrily grabbed its soundbite for broadcast to the breakfast audience who'd been bidding cash pledges to the website all morning. It was over, it was wonderful, we had our media coverage and we had our publicity. The Wheel of Hope had delivered.

Back on safe ground, I was casting around for other ideas to try and build up the donations for the charity, when I suddenly thought about holding a fashion show. When I thought a bit more about it, I thought how lovely it would be to ask my

WeightWatchers ladies to be the models. The idea caught and burned brightly and the most incredible bunch of people got involved. My WeightWatchers leader Vera, who was also becoming a firm friend, basically took over, picked up the ball and ran with it. We asked for help from our local hotel, the Crowne Plaza in Blanchardstown, and they gave us their beautiful ballroom and a stage for the show. The local Draíocht Theatre gave us a spotlight and Ballyfermot College of Further Education provided us with a camera crew and lights operators. My friend and work colleague Siobhan O'Connor, the Gossip Girl at 98FM, agreed to be my MC and 98FM DJs Barry Dunne and Darragh O'Dea took on the task of organising sound and music. They were all wonderful and Barry recorded a really great music track that took account of all the separate themes we were running in the show. Diageo provided us with a drinks reception and the best goodie bags in town and we had amazing spot prizes from the great and the good of business and showbiz. Too many people helped to all be listed here, but it was absolutely incredible to see how generous people really are. More than that, the night was a powerful testament to women and everyone was truly impressed by the positivity that pulsated from the stage.

The WeightWatchers ladies were absolutely stunning—and their very special escorts added a real wow factor. Again it was one of those things that just seemed to develop as the plan unfolded. As a journalist I wanted to pay tribute to some of the amazing unsung heroes who help me every day in my work and I thought of putting together a mixed band from the Defence Forces, Gardaí, Fire Brigade, HSE Paramedics and Coast Guard to join us on the catwalk on the night. To my surprise and pleasure they all agreed and the lads were absolutely wonderful. It was a pleasure to highlight them too and the audience warmly applauded both their performance on the night and also the knowledge that these lads and their female colleagues put their lives on the line for all of us at a moment's notice. As with the 'Cars at the Castle' event, I would have been a lot more reluctant to commit to doing a fashion show if I had the slightest idea of how much organisation would be involved. Again, beginner's luck and total ignorance were my best aids—that and the astonishing power of people inspired to do good for those less fortunate than themselves.

During the fundraising part of the Everest trip, there were many people who challenged me about why I wasn't fundraising for charities at home. The truth is there are many deserving charities and I'd love to help them all—but I don't recognise boundaries or borders when it comes to love and compassion. I'm honoured to have had the opportunity to help children in Kolkata who are so desperately deserving of our help. On this occasion, fate happened to bring

The Hope Foundation to my door and I will always be eternally grateful. I set out trying to do something good or give something back or say thank you for the gifts I had received. I ended up realising that helping others is a sure way of helping yourself. The more I give, the more I receive; it's like a tide that can't be stemmed. Happiness is the best possible reward in life and I'm happy to help.

I don't know if I'm religious but I believe I am spiritual. While I've always laughed at 'fakey reiki' and crystals and moonbeams, I don't discount those beliefs completely and I have to admit there are certain tides and currents in the universe that I simply can't explain. Perhaps losing Mum heightened those feelings and maybe in mourning we reach out for answers as a way to help temper our grief, I really don't know. But there certainly seemed to be coincidences and portents during this year that I couldn't really explain or ignore. I referred to them as 'rings and roundabouts'—meaning that certain truths kept repeating themselves until they were noticed. One such incident involved the fashion show. It's a tiny thing, not of much significance to others perhaps, but so powerfully felt by me that I must mention it.

The WeightWatchers ladies were being fitted out in all the gorgeous fashions that Debenhams were providing us with for the show and there was huge excitement about fittings and rehearsals. Remember, along with their appetite for style and fashion and pretty things to wear, these ladies had the additional element of coming from a place where they had previously found it difficult to find pretty clothes to wear in their sizes. They had come from a place where they perhaps didn't find themselves attractive to look at, and there were almost certainly a number—myself included—who had a few question marks about their body image. Now they were to model high fashion in front of a paying audience of 500 guests, they were being dressed by a personal shopper and they would be out on a catwalk strutting their stuff across a 3-hour show. You can imagine how that could be both exciting and daunting; in fact it could be plain terrifying. Personally, I kept out of the style arrangements. I knew I had to model as part of the show and I would be helping with the overall presentation, but I was too busy with arranging different aspects of the show with Vera, my co-conspirator, planning running orders, selling tickets and holding down a full-time job, to spend much time thinking about how I'd look or what I'd be wearing—or maybe I was just in denial and avoiding the terror of thinking about that catwalk! There was also the issue of mourning; it had been six months since my mum had died, and until then I had continued to wear black as a mark of respect. It was an old-fashioned thing to do, but it felt right to me at the time. Now I had decided to put mourning aside for the charity and wear colour again. I felt I was doing the right thing, but I might still have been a little uncomfortable or uncertain about the idea. Anyway the end result was that I told WeightWatchers and Debenhams to go ahead and put their selection for me together themselves and I'd just come in briefly for a quick fitting the day before and take what I got.

Racing across the city to Blanchardstown after work the day before the show, I had no thoughts at all about what I'd be wearing, other than that I hoped the clothes would fit, because I didn't have much time for them to pick up new selections. I parked, sprinted into Debenhams and was thrilled when I started trying on all the pretty dresses they had lined up for me. Finally they went to pull the rail for the ballgown section and Ann Peppard, the personal shopper, swung around with a beautiful, rich, glamorous dress on a hanger. 'It's got to be the red,' she said—and I burst into tears. They were the exact words my mum had spoken to me about the dress for the Hope Ball the night before she died. Probably coincidence, but for me at that moment, it was my mum speaking to me and telling me it was okay to wear colour again, it was okay to go to Everest and I was pretty much doing everything okay. I'd had doubts that I hadn't even realised until that moment, but they washed away in a flood of tears in the Debenhams changing room the night before the Hope Counts Fashion Show.

The finale for the fashion show had another surprise in store under the theme 'from walking your dog to walking a mountain'. We had started the show with casual and sportswear, moving on through various themes of new designs and party wear, before ending up with the entire Hope/Everest team on stage in full mountaineering kit: boots, helmets and ice axes, led out by the man himself who'd driven up from Kerry especially for the occasion. Pat Falvey greeted the crowd to thunderous applause as he gave his own infamous motivational speech about summiting Mount Everest and how everyone has their own mountain to climb. The positive energy in the room was enough to move mountains. The night was a huge success, topping off our best efforts and raising my total from the hoped-for €6,000 to a massive €21,000—showing that even in a recession, people's generosity is absolutely astounding.

Chapter 8
Peaking in Kerry

We've just a few weeks to go and the time is really running out. Very shortly I'm going to have to ease back on the hard training, to build strength for the actual expedition. I'm afraid I haven't done enough and wish I had even one more month. My weight's down to around 12.5 stone, which is great, after coming from 23 stone—but I'd really hoped to break the 12 and I haven't quite managed it. I'm strong, I know I'm strong, but Pat said last time I was down in Kerry that I lacked speed . . . and I still think I lack speed. We're heading down there shortly, the whole Hope team, for our final assessment.

Celebrities or not, we've all been working our socks off to be ready for Pat's eagle eye. Jenny's been really brave, she suffered a leg injury hiking in Bray and ended up in plaster and on crutches, but she's come back from that and is running again. We're all close to being mentally exhausted, which isn't a good place to be. We've all been fundraising flat out and event management is tough enough without coming at it as a complete newcomer and amateur. Trying to think of ideas and execute them, to organise the event, the tickets, the flyers, the insurance, hoping and dreading that people will turn up. It's really brutally hard and I've acquired a huge respect for people who do this sort of thing all the time.

On top of the fundraising we have all the press coverage, TV and radio interviews, the time it takes to plan them, agreeing on what everyone is saying, when to release photos and when not to, so that all our separate campaigns don't collide, then the stress of actually doing them. Then we have our training, which is really five days a week in the gym—and at least three days a week out on a hill. All of this on top of full-time jobs. We can't get days off to catch up with expedition work. It wouldn't be fair and besides, most of our vacation time is being eaten up by the actual expedition, which will take up to three weeks. It's a major undertaking and even though I appreciated the enormity of the task right from the start, it's still a huge shock to the system. Sleep is an optional extra at this stage. So it's a slightly less giddy crew that find themselves back on the train to Killarney to face the final assessment at the Mountain Lodge.

We pour off the train to meet the bus to the Lodge on Friday night; as ever, there's a complicated assortment of boots and rucksacks and climbing sticks and ice-picks all falling out around us. Still big grins and warm hugs, even though it's all a bit muted. Arriving in Beaufort we're not sure if we're relieved or disappointed to see no trace of tents this time. We've graduated to the house, the power showers and plush beds. We dump our gear and head to the now familiar Kate's. Strains of traditional music greet us as we pull up and I can smell the distinctive aroma of turf in the air around me as we fall out into the Gap. As usual Pat regales us all with stories of icy adventures and his next ambition to walk to the North Pole with Dr Clare O'Leary, the first Irish woman to summit Everest. If they make it, they'll have made it together to the North and South Poles and to the top of Everest; the so-called three Poles—in honour of those explorers/adventurers who went before them. Our spirits lift and before long the team is back in high form, eating and drinking and looking forward to the day ahead.

The day starts early with a lecture on gear, what we'll need to get us to Base Camp and what some of us will need to bring us further to Island Peak and the extreme conditions that can be found at 20,305 ft. Equipment expert, renowned rock-climber, environmentalist and writer Con Moriarty joins Pat's team at the Mountain Lodge and gives us an amazing presentation on gear, its function and any possible failings. Outside the stone-built front of Pat's Mountain Lodge, Con has set up trestle tables with endless supplies of gear and harnesses and clips and carabiners and devices that are totally unfamiliar to me, despite my sessions at the Trinity climbing wall. Con is an amazing character and we watch captivated during the briefing. Physically, he's an imposing man—of large stature and with wild looks that seem totally married to the mountainous terrain that surrounds us as we stand on Pat's lawn looking at the unfamiliar lines of equipment in front of us. Con's been running cables onto the wall of the Lodge and the knuckle of one of his hands is skinned and bleeding where he knocked it against the roughened stone. I stare transfixed and a sense of unreality hits me as Con talks in detail about what the three-layer system is all about, the wicking, the warmth and the wet-resistance layers that are the starting point for any climber going out on any hill in any country. He shows us the difference between equipment and clothing that looks sporty but falls apart under pressure or offers very little protection . . . and equipment that does the job and is designed for the type of conditions we'll be encountering. He produces a boot, roughly hewn in half across the sole, to show us the insulating layers and the protections that might save us from losing toes or worse. I feel as if I'm looking at my life and it's on the Discovery Channel.

This hostile terrain that we're talking about, these wild mountains that surround us here, the warrior-type gear merchant who's showing us the ropes —literally—I suddenly find a rush of excitement and energy overtaking me. My God, I'm going to Everest.

Con and Pat go through all our expedition gear, which we've lugged down from Dublin and up from Cork on demand and have assembled outside on the lawn. We discuss what we've got, what works, what we might need to add, what we should take out and leave behind. Great debate follows on the boots and the types of crampons that we might use on the ice. The hiking boots for Everest Base Camp must be sturdy and reliable, waterproof and with good ankle support. However, for any of the team pushing on to Island Peak, entirely new and very expensive boots are vital. They need to be specially insulated against temperatures as low as -30° Celsius, and they need to be 'double-booted' with an inner sleeve that can be removed and dried separate to the outer shell. These boots were traditionally developed to have a hard plastic casing—like ski boots—and are still referred to as 'plastic boots'. Pat shows the attention to detail which has earned him a reputation as one of the best expedition planners in the world. Nothing is left to chance; everything is decided upon on the ground outside the Lodge, then labelled and tagged and itemised and re-packed. We are amateurs but we have the firm conviction that this man not only knows what he is doing, but is determined that we will know too. To us, this journey may have started as a celebrity challenge, but I realise standing here that regardless of our own stories and personal motivations, Pat is clearly in the business of building proficient, self-reliant climbers. We're not just being handed a bag of gear, we're taught why we've got it, what it does, what we need to use it for, and any alternative uses. Whether we like it or not, he is dragging us into a level of competency that we never expected at the start. I'm impressed and enthusiastic to learn all I can from both of these incredibly experienced adventurers.

After the technical briefing and a quick lunch inside the Mountain Lodge, we head back outside for instruction on ice-work, how to walk across snow and ice and how to try and prevent ourselves from hurtling down a glacier into a crevasse. Getting to Everest Base Camp at well over 17,500 ft is no mean feat, but pushing beyond that into the icy domain of Island Peak leaves behind any last vestige of being on just a hike or trek and brings with it very real danger. The team is quickly realising that pushing ahead to this level demands that each member take responsibility for their own safety, as a single slip could not only put themselves but their colleagues at risk.

We lace into plastic boots and snap on crampons and climb into the harness. Then we unbuckle the harness, snap off the crampons and start all over again . . . and again. We're being timed and we knock nearly a minute off the time it takes us to kit up, before Pat is finally satisfied to move on to the next step. He explains the exercise is vital and we must continue to practise at home. We're clocking about 2.15 minutes and he tells us to get that time down to 90 seconds. If we meet ice and need to put crampons on, we've got to be able to do it efficiently in the dark or in storm conditions, with gloves and mitts on if necessary. Delays on the ice mean lost fingers, lost toes, and lost lives.

For the rest of the day, whenever I was slow at an exercise, Pat would stop near my ear and comment, 'Jenny's freezing, Rob's frostbitten, George is dead' . . . with increasing pace, until I finished my task. It got extremely annoying, but the lesson would stay with me later when I needed it.

Finally booted with crampons snapped securely in place and ice axes in hand, the team of adventurers headed off to do damage, up the path to a grassy knoll at the back of the Lodge. We trekked up the steps and discovered how awkward it felt to move across wood and gravel and clay with spikes protruding from our toes. Up on the bank we were drilled on how to walk up and down a slope with crampons on, with the ice-pick always held in the hand facing higher up the mountain, in readiness to stop a fall. Finally we were told to drop to the ground and use the ice axes to anchor ourselves. Laughing, we hit the deck and looked around to see a very silly-looking bunch of celebrities looking goofily across the grass at each other in various degrees of lopsidedness. Pat and Con explained the mechanics of breaking a fall on ice. They explained that falling on ice in waterproofs is like taking a plastic refuse sack out at Christmas and using it as a sleigh to slide down a local snowy hill at speed. It was an innocent enough image, but they went on to explain that even when the group is tied together, a falling climber can take the whole line with them, if they pick up speed and go crashing into a crevasse. We listened intently as we learned that the ice axe needs to be used in a sharp stabbing motion, like braking in a car, to try and create traction and slow the fall. If you whack it into the ice, it's likely to jump back and throw you off the mountain. If you don't make it stick, you keep sliding. There's a balance to getting it right. In the meantime, we needed to bend our legs up at the knees to stop the crampons sticking in the ice and somersaulting us over our own backs. It was hardcore stuff we were hearing here and it was scary. We practised for about an hour on a sunny day on a grassy hill at the back of Pat's house. It was no replacement for working on snow or ice, but it was all we had.

The sun disappeared behind a cloud, just around the time we bussed up and started heading down the Gap to go abseiling with Con and Pat. I was back on familiar territory here. I'd done plenty of hiking in the Gap of Dunloe over the summer so felt I knew where we were and I'd abseiled the Wheel of Dublin without coming a cropper, so an abseil in the lovely Gap, close to the road in the middle of the afternoon, would be child's play . . . and it was. I was giggling with enthusiasm after the first drop. We were all getting a couple of goes with Pat monitoring safety for the descent and Con taking charge of the rope work and the drops. I couldn't resist but hopped back up the hill to the top of the cliff again to get another go. It was when Con turned around and spotted my grin behind him for the third time that he realised my game. 'You're back again for more,' he laughed and, grinning, I moved forward to get tied in again. I couldn't resist it. Con decided it was time to take the safety off and left me in control of my own descent. I'd been up and down the climbing wall in Trinity lots at this stage and was totally in my comfort zone, so I dropped over the edge, happily abseiling my way to the bottom, to run back up the hill, ready to go again. I squeezed in lots more abseils that afternoon. The sun and the bitter biting little midges came out, but I didn't care. I was in my element and picking up tips on braking and hanging from Con, who's reputed to be one of the best climbers in the country. It was joy on a rope. We were all comfortable on the ropes by the end of the day and headed back to Kate's that evening again to debrief over good food and a few drinks. It was good.

Kerry threw a dirty day at us next morning, as if it knew we were heading to the big one. Carrauntoohil faded behind the mist as we booted up and pulled the waterproofs from our pack. I knew a time-trial was likely at some stage today, because Pat had to make the final decision on who was going to Base Camp, and who—if anyone—would be ready for an attempt on Island Peak. We were going to be wet and cold; that was obvious. But despite being the slowest in the group, as we headed off to the hills I again felt I had an advantage. I'd been doing my homework on these hills, I'd been out on the mountains every spare moment I had, and I had trekked down to Kerry whenever I had a free weekend. I reckoned I had a feeling for Ireland's biggest mountain, I had put in the hours in the gym, I was stronger than I'd ever been in my life, I'd been walking in heavy, rigid, Boreal boots all summer in an attempt to build my leg muscles and to improve the art of actually walking across rough terrain and 'edging' or cutting into the scree with the side of my boot. I'd soaked up all the tips I could from other mountain men and women about ways to place your foot when walking uphill and how to breathe and how to control your temperature. I pulled my hood on and stepped out of the van to be hit by a wave of wind and water, and I smiled. I was ready.

The World Wide Adventure Team had one last lesson for us. We needed to practise fixed-rope techniques to prepare us for climbing the icy headwall at Island Peak, and we needed to practise walking tied together, for when the team would be crossing a glacier or ice-field. In the mist and rain I again had absolutely no idea where we were going, and I was again irritated at my lack of co-ordination or navigation skills. There simply wasn't the time to learn any extra tricks with all that still had to be done before we left but I promised myself that when I got back from Nepal, I would sign up for a Mountain Skills course and learn how to read a map. It irritated me that I wasn't self-sufficient on a mountain and the more time I spent on the hills, the more I realised that I wanted the freedom of being able to head off on my own to explore instead of always relying on someone to guide me and call the shots. As it happened, we were heading up for an early hike over the MacGillicuddy Reeks. Conditions were brutal, wet and windy with mist so closed in we could hardly see the line ahead. We pushed on, and my mantra 'one foot in front of the other' was put to good use as we pulled our chins under our hoods and got stuck in. Conversation was impossible; the wind would grasp the words from our mouths and hurl them away if we ever spared the breath to form them. On a fine day it would have been a spectacular ascent to a section of the main ridge of the Reeks, the Coimín na Péiste arête, between Cruach Mhor and Cnoc na Péiste, but in these conditions, in the shadow of the 'Big Gun', it was brutal and challenging. We scrambled over boulders and craggy shafts of rock with enormous drops below and practised coiling ropes between us, using fang-like outcrops as protection in case one of us were to slip. The team was tense, wet, cold, apprehensive and downright unhappy. To my amazement, I was in my element. For once, speed wasn't an issue. The weather was a leveller and I really felt like a strong link in the chain for the first time. I knew my ropes; I knew how to get the best out of my gear, to squeeze an extra inch of shelter from the wind when I got the chance. I kept snacking from the nuts in my pocket to keep my energy up, and drank frequently from the Platypus water system in my rucksack. I was living the dream and loving the moment. This was a mountain and this was me and I could have happily stayed out in this all day.

We dropped slightly down off the ridge to a platform at the foot of a slab, later uniformly referred to as 'a dirty great slab in the middle of a soaking wet Kerry dream'. Pat and Con set up a fixed rope and began our exercise for the headwall on Island Peak. The wind howled around the ridge, but this spot had some shelter and the rain had eased slightly. The group was tense and quiet, nerves had been stretched tight, crossing over the torturous craggy ridge with the clearly visible drops below. All were thinking about how the return journey would go, and whether it would involve the same passage. I knew it did, I'd been here before, but I knew we'd get through it with Pat and Con at the helm. My first trek along the Reeks had involved a 10-hour hike in less severe weather but without a rope, so today I felt spoiled in comparison.

Con disappeared up the slab, free climbing and showing a clean pair of heels and total knowledge of the rock and the ridge, and it was so impressive to see movement like that. I was incredibly jealous of his talent and strength and natural ability. He tied on and threw down rope to Pat at the base, and between them they set up a fixed line and asked who—if any of us— wanted to tie on. Philip Gray went first, I think, and Rob Ross next. I was watching the lads and dying to try it, but somehow I doubted myself. The tension in the group seemed to suggest this was hardcore and I was picking up the vibes and yet I looked again and felt I wanted to have a shot. There were no grips on the slab, it was sloping and wet and slippery and the lads were sliding and cracking off it. I remember wondering if I could brace my feet on the rock and push off against them with the jumar ascender clamped onto the rope. I was running options in my mind and I wanted to have a go, but I still hesitated. There were a lot of cold people on the natural rocky platform and there was slowness in the next candidate coming forward.

Pat suggested that we should pack up and call it a day and, horrified, I knew I couldn't let him take the slab away from me. 'What if I go up and get stuck half-way?' I said.

Pat looked at me quietly and replied, 'We'd have to initiate a rescue to get you down, which we could do, but people will get cold and hypothermia could set in, it's very bad weather to suffer that sort of delay.'

I looked again at the slab. 'Can I brace my feet, flat-footed, off the slab?' I asked.

'You can,' he quietly replied.

'Can I use the jumar to help me push up the rope?'

'You can,' he said.

'I want to try.'

'Off you go so,' said Pat.

I tied my harness onto the safety and clipped my jumar to the fixed rope and began to climb. I'm sure it was the least elegant performance in the Kerry mountains that day. I'm sure I slapped my knees off the slab a million times and relied far too much on the rope. I'm sure it looked absolutely painful—but I thought I was flying, and, as I pulled through the mist over a small overhang at the top, Con raised down a hand to help me up and shouted in delight, 'Fair play to you, girl,' and a few other compliments which, grinning ear to ear, I was keen to accept as my right! Before heading back to Dublin I asked Pat again about Island Peak. 'You don't have the speed, girl,' he said. Then added, 'But you better pack the plastic boots.'

Chapter 9
A Trip to Shangri-La

Day 1—Pat's blog—Kathmandu Start of Hope Everest Expedition: 1 October 2010

No matter how many times I go to Nepal, I get excited at the thought of returning to my spiritual home. A place that has changed my life, having gone there in 1991 on an expedition to climb a beautiful mountain known as Ama Dablam with a group of good friends. I went first, as the cliché goes, to 'find myself', only to lose myself and return to civilisation a new person. A lifetime later, I have been here 25 times and I have never lost the joy of returning to this amazing country. Its sights, sounds, smells and the hustle and bustle of a vibrant community of people; to once again experience their culture as I lead a group of Irish adventurers on an exciting journey to explore what is for them, their Everest. For me, it is another return to my most favourite place on planet earth. Mixing adventure with a spiritual odyssey and to meet old friends that I have made over the years, with a group of enthusiastic new volunteers who are helping to make life better for the street children of Kolkata by raising money to enhance their life through education.

So we were finally here. We had embarked on our expedition to Nepal, to climb to Base Camp Mount Everest and perhaps beyond, for The Hope Foundation. The flight from Dublin to Dubai was uneventful, although I was excited to be flying through UAE airspace and fascinated to see the luxury of the mosaic and design at the airport when we landed, although there was no time to go outside. One of those typical airport transit drops, where you tuck yourself away in the travel lounge and try to make the best of it. Some of the team slept for a while in adjoining bunk rooms, which was a novelty for me, but something I didn't bother actually using because I was too excited to sleep. I tried some of the food from the amazing buffet, still mindful of diet—even at this dramatic stage of my journey, my new habits held true. But there was an astonishing selection of beautiful fruit that I dipped into, and some interesting new flavours that I hadn't experienced before. Then I turned to the computer room and thought I'd blog a bit and file to the radio station back at home. I recorded the radio piece and sent it by email, but gave up on the blog, as the Internet connection seemed to be fired. Communications were definitely going to be an issue on the mountain. I had promised to record radio links back to work when possible and to blog to 98FM and to Pat Falvey's corporate web page, but actually getting internet access to email the material was likely to be limited, so I'd decided I would blog every day, and send batches when I could. Pat and I were sharing minutes on a satellite phone, so that we could both record radio interviews, and so that he could contact his Kerry HQ, where Niall and Lorraine in his office would keep our families updated with our progress. Rob Ross and Jenny Kavanagh were filing reports back to RTÉ. Finally, our second flight was called, and we began the final stage to Kathmandu.

Day 2—Teena's blog—Lukla

Today I flew into a mountain. From Kathmandu, Pat hired a small twin-engined propeller plane and we flew into Lukla, a village hanging off a Nepalese mountain, and the next step on our journey to Mount Everest. The tiny runway is buried in the mountain and the arrival has to be the scariest air approach in the world. The plane's engines took on an almost animal-like pitch as she

*turned in towards the cliff, and after watching the
pilot bless himself . . . so did I. Brakes and reverse
thrusters kicked in almost the moment the wheels
touched down and within moments we were out
and standing on a mountain. A quiet crowd of
Lukla locals gathered around us, with hardly a
murmur, their quiet presence a marked contrast
from the wall of noise we'd met when getting off
our international flight in Kathmandu the day
before. We walked to a nearby teahouse for lunch
and already some of us were feeling the effects of
the altitude. We had flown in at 9,000 ft, almost
three times the height of Carrauntoohil, Ireland's
highest mountain. Shortly afterwards, we put our
day packs on our backs and started walking—
downhill. Our destination is Phakding, 1,000 ft
below. The plan is to 'walk high and sleep low' to
help adjust to altitude. It means walking to a
certain height, then coming back down a little,
before re-tracing our steps the next day. As the days
of walking and climbing accumulate, I just know
that's going to be annoying! Onwards and
upwards . . .*

It was such a strange new world. Despite reading and
googling about Nepal for months, the reality was
hard to prepare for and hard to explain. Of course I
must have been excited by the prospect of what lay
ahead. I was probably running high on adrenaline

and it was strange to be away from work for three weeks, for the first time since I was 17. All of those considerations were probably clouding my thinking, but I swear I felt close to heaven there. I imagined the air smelled of herbs, and the rivers and insects sang together in a constant low chant that separated day and night. It was like walking through a kaleidoscopic land of colour and harmony, with farmers carrying on their daily life around us, as we passed through the lush vegetation. I knew this part of Nepal would be warm and rich in colour and life, but I simply wasn't prepared for this. In Lukla I came face to face with our yaks for the first time; these long-haired beasts would carry the bulk of our equipment and provisions up the mountain and the bells knocking metallically around their necks would add to the chorus of the mountain. I watched as the porters struggled to lift the dark green 'Pat Falvey' branded kitbags onto their flanks, slinging down low on either side of their narrow spines, and I thought for a moment of the ridges we'd be climbing in the weeks ahead. Certainly the dark green panniers would leave no doubt that this was 'the Irish group'. Already Pat was being saluted in the street. It's amazing how well known he is here. He has challenged and won passage from Chomolungma or Goddess Mother Earth twice, claiming the summit of Everest from both North and South, and that affords him status and respect. Seeing the adventurer in this environment gave him an added sense of dignity; his affection and respect for these people and this region were palpable and touching and seemed at odds with the commercial, hard-nosed businessman that I'd come to know in recent months. I know he's a showman, but this is genuine and real. He cares.

Day 3—Teena's blog—Namche Bazaar

Today was tough. I climbed 3,000 ft and it hurt. But it was extraordinary and I loved it. We woke at 6 a.m. at Phakding and breakfasted on fried potatoes and eggs in the shadow of the mountain. A snow-capped peak burned pink and golden as the sun rose. It isn't Everest, we won't glimpse her until tomorrow, but it's stunning, and a reminder of the icy treks ahead. Here at 8,000 ft, it's hot and we're walking through lush green after the recent monsoons, though temperatures plunge as soon as the sun sets. Our trek today took us past beautiful rivers and waterfalls, with rainbows shimmering in the spray. We crossed narrow suspension bridges moving dramatically with the span and our 14-strong team trooping across. I found them scary and I met them far too frequently for comfort. 8 hours climbing today. Altitude kicked in a little. I had a small nosebleed and felt lightheaded if I moved too fast; but getting a rhythm helped and walking into Namche Bazaar felt great, if somewhat tempered by the knowledge that we were staying in a tea lodge far beyond the town. Uphill of course!

When we flew into Lukla, Rob Ross turned to me just minutes after getting off the plane and asked if I could feel the altitude and the thin air. I couldn't and I thought maybe Rob was imagining it, because we'd been worrying about it for so long. I was wrong, of course; my ignorance was kicking in, just as Rob's reaction to the thinning oxygen was. George felt it too and Jenny, but certainly Rob looked concerned and apprehensive. I still didn't know what he was talking about and surmised that I should just be grateful that I hadn't felt anything and leave it at that. I did ask what it felt like and he said he felt dizzy or light-headed. I didn't feel anything at Lukla, but the following day I got a touch of a reaction as we climbed 3,000 ft to Namche Bazaar. It was still very minor but I noticed when walking that the ground seemed to move at a different speed to me. I've never been into chemicals, but I imagine this is how I'd feel if I was high. Then at dinner I noticed my nose was bleeding and I knew I was feeling it. I was relieved to see the nosebleed though. When I was a little girl, I always had a nosebleed at the beginning and end of a cold, and my mum used to tell me it was releasing pressure in my brain! I've no idea if that's scientifically true or not, my knowledge of anatomy is starkly lacking, but it felt reassuring to me and I grasped at her old words from long ago and wrapped them around me like a shawl.

Altitude aside, I think the walk to Namche that second day was one of the toughest for me, although I never admitted it to anyone. I was panicking a little bit. It was simply a trail through the mountains, largely hewn out of stone and pretty much paved or at least worn to a path the whole way up, but it was unrelenting, it kept going up and up, with no levelling off, and of course I had no idea how long we would be walking for, because that depended on our speed. I had fallen into place in an odd kind of position, two-thirds of the way down the group. I walked at my own pace as I'd been advised by all my hiking and mountaineering friends, not trying to speed up or slow down to match with the other walkers around me. Perhaps it's my short legs, but I never seemed to match anyone else's gait. I wasn't isolating myself—I've thought about it, and I really don't think that's the case—but a pattern quickly emerged that saw me walking pretty much on my own. I loved the other members of the team, and these days I consider them to be among my family, but when it came to walking I just seemed to fall into step alone. That third day, I found that tough.

Day 4—Teena's blog—Ama Dablam

If you left Dublin today and flew in to join me, you would probably die. I'm at 12,000 ft and you can't breathe here unless you've had a chance to acclimatise. Today is a rest day which means we only walked for a couple of hours and gained 1,000 ft. After lunch, we turn around and head right back down to Namche. It's a chance for us to prepare our heart and lungs for the next push tomorrow, when we've got another tough day's climbing. Today we had a special treat. At 12,000 ft we stopped for lunch at a Nepalese Hotel and Extreme Artist Philip Gray gave us an art lesson. We hope to paint at Base Camp and auction the canvas later for The Hope Foundation. Today we each used pastels to create a picture of the beautiful iconic mountain, Ama Dablam. It marks the gateway to Everest; and yes, today we saw those snow-capped peaks for the very first time . . .

That blog caused a bit of controversy at home and caused me a bit of scolding when I got back, from relatives who were totally alarmed by my reference to death! It was inspired by a story doing the rounds about an airplane runway that used to exist on the mountain above Namche, where Japanese generals flew in guests to stay in Nepal, only to find they suffered from the effects of arriving unprepared at

12,000 ft. The airstrip at Shyangboche certainly existed, but I've been unable to document unfortunate deaths for Japanese tourists. It was another 1,000 ft above Namche, but as rest days go, this was a good one. The acclimatisation walk felt easy compared to the long slog up to Namche the previous day, which had really taken its toll on me. But today I got my confidence back and practically skipped back down later that day, despite rough terrain on the descent. I was good on the downward stretches, partially because I'd put in so much time working on it. Because I'd carried 23 stone on my knees for so long, I was always concerned they'd be the first place I'd carry an injury, so I'd worked hard on building up the muscles around the joint. There's a set of steps over at Spink Mountain in Wicklow that I spent many an afternoon climbing up and down . . . and now it was paying off. It may sound like a pretty minor talent, but when you're climbing at altitude you do a lot of acclimatising walks, which obviously means going up and down. It hadn't occurred to me that the down-work would have been such a benefit to me, but now I was reaping some unexpected rewards.

The day at Shyangboche was also memorable for artistic reasons. Philip Gray is dubbed the 'Extreme Artist' because he travels to extreme places on the planet and paints. He's painted on the Icelandic volcano at the centre of the ash-cloud, he's painted underwater and now he'd revealed to us that he was going to try and paint at Island Peak. Pat wasn't convinced and warned him that he'd have to find some way to use pastels with mitts, because he'd get frostbite if he left his gloves off at 20,000 ft. There was some debate, which clearly was not going to be settled until we got there—if we got there! That day Philip taught us to paint! He said he could do it and we all laughed at him, but there at the foothills of that incredibly beautiful mountain Ama Dablam we all used pastels and canvas and created 'masterpieces' that rather shocked us all. They were beautiful. They weren't picture postcards or photostatic representations, but they were art and they were gorgeous. As my beautiful Ama Dablam emerged from the canvas, I thought of Con Moriarty, the 'gear maestro' we'd met back in The Gap in Kerry, whose amazing Boreal boots had brought me up this far. Con had told me to look out for Ama Dablam as one of his favourite peaks. He'd also given me some extremely important advice as I left Dublin Airport; he told me to forget about summits and success and take the time to see the beautiful country I was walking through. It was nice to take a moment to remember new friends in such a beautiful place.

Day 5—Pat's blog—Tengboche and Deboche: 5 October 2010

This morning we trekked with fantastic views towards our next stop Tengboche. We decended to the valley floor and rose through the forest to Tengboche and the well-known Buddhist monastery there. Jenny has some issues with her knee but is moving along okay. We arrived at 3 p.m. and received a special blessing (Puja) from over 60 monks, emotional for all of the team. We descended later in darkness to arrive in Deboche at 6.30 p.m. A good aul sing-along was had by the whole team. Along the way we had stunning views of the mighty Everest behind Lhotse-Nuptse wall. In Deboche we start to circle under Ama Dablam as it towers over us. Tomorrow we start for Pheriche.

Day 5—Teena's blog—Tengboche and Deboche

Today I kneeled in a cold temple for two hours and tried to meditate. It was a hard day's climbing through hot sun, from Namche to Deboche. The whole team did well though, as we cranked up the acclimatisation another notch. Jenny's knee hurts, but she's still doing okay. Under the shadow of Everest we passed through an ancient gateway to the town that hosts the local monastery. We spent several hours listening to the monks' ceremonial chanting and were blessed for the journey ahead. Without exception, we all found it a moving experience. I jogged down the pathway afterwards feeling special . . . invincible. Then my foot slipped, and my ankle turned. It hurt—disaster! I hopped to a nearby mountain stream, kicked off my boot and plunged my foot in. It was dark, and the light from my head torch drew a circle around my foot and the icy river. As the rest of the group sought shelter in a nearby teahouse, the sound of silence descended. Within moments I was picking up new sounds, rustles and creaks in the darkness beyond. My memory turned to the joking jibes at dinner the night before about snakes and poison spiders. I stood the terrors and the cold for a few minutes more, before bolting for the teahouse 'with a tiger on my tail'. Tomorrow's walk is tough, but I'll deal with that tomorrow. Tonight, I'm safe and warm and that will do for now.

The tiger was imaginary, but the injuries weren't. Both Jenny and I were now carrying problems while Rob was suffering badly with headaches and general sickness. We felt strange, because we were knackered, but yet that day was such a special day after our trip to the monastery at Tengboche. I'd never felt such strong spirituality and it'd affected us all. We could hardly speak for a while; we were all terribly overwhelmed with individual feelings that are hard to explain. I actually felt upset for a while, but had no idea why. I sound like a fruitcake but the energy around the temple seemed disturbing to me. Part of my yoga routine is a short 'moving meditation' which I continued every morning and night, wherever we were staying on the mountain, but I'd never been any good at pure meditation. Yet in the monastery we sat for hours and in that place it seemed easy to empty the mind and clear the spirit. We only meant to stay about a half an hour, but we just couldn't seem to drag ourselves away, and Pat was in no hurry either. We also had a very moving ceremony where these monks who knew nothing about us granted us a special blessing for our journey ahead. Leaving the monastery, I felt perhaps that I had undergone a sort of 'soft reboot', the sort you apply to your computer with Control/Alt/Delete, and perhaps that's why I felt such temporary sadness and disturbance. Anyway I picked myself up and started to jog through the darkness to Deboche, which I stupidly paid for by twisting my ankle. Costly, dim, dopey mistake; I was seriously annoyed with myself, but I did what I could to make up for the slip. I put the foot in freezing water, popped an anti-inflammatory and strapped the ankle well before bed. I could only wait and see. In contrast, we had popcorn at dinner—which felt like the biggest treat ever—and I dragged out my guitar and initiated the best sing-song of the trip. Not bad when you consider that I can't play guitar! A poor

Sherpa hauled it the whole way up the mountain because I was determined that I'd find someone on the trip who could play—and tonight I did. We ended up with an international concert running between groups of Australian, American, English and Japanese trekkers all heading either up or down the mountain, and the fabulous George McMahon led us through the best version of 'Bohemian Rhapsody' that I have EVER heard. Pat Falvey has that on video somewhere and we have GOT to get it back!

Day 6—Teena's blog—Pheriche

Today I hit a wall . . . but I climbed over it . . . After yesterday's adventures, I struggled to keep up with Team Hope, as I limped my way up a mountain. It was another tough ascent, rising up 1,500 ft for over five hours. The terrain was rough and each leap from boulder to boulder jarred my injured foot. There was no other option but to keep on walking and I gritted my teeth and got on with it. I admit I felt sorry for myself, I even felt a couple of tears well up at times. The team is fabulous though, with lots of hugs on tap, and the scenery helped to distract me. The turning point was when we all burst into song, winding our way through the mountains like the Von Trapps and bursting into giggles whenever we met groups of climbers on the way down. Maybe it's the altitude, but we've got to be the happiest group of trekkers out here and we've painted smiles on strangers' faces from here to Shangri-La ... Team Hope's Birthday boy David Walshe later commented that we'd sent smiles around the World. Celebrating Dave's birthday with pizza later that night, at 14,000 ft, life again felt good.

Day 6—Pat's blog—Pheriche: 7 October 2010

All arrived well at Pheriche where the team will start to move above the flora and into the tundra. More tomorrow.

Pheriche is a funny old place. The name means 'a wilderness', but it's not. A quick walk up into the hills above the valley shows that area is traditionally a stronghold for farming, but back in the valley, the river Tsola sweeps past a settlement of new and modern buildings, clearly showing the marks that trekking and the outside world have gouged on tradition. I don't like it. I know we shouldn't expect citizens of any nation to live in a museum for the entertainment of foreigners, but I just felt uncomfortable at how deep and jagged the newness of everything is in this community. It has a lot to be proud of, including a volunteer-run hospital and research facility with daily lectures explaining the dangers of Acute Mountain Sickness, for those who would like to be informed and are willing to make a small donation; there are also a wonderful new hostel and surrounding buildings that clearly show a tourist trade that keeps the local workforce well occupied. But I'm still not convinced about it. Then again, I'm probably just being selfish, wanting to keep that wonderful Nepalese spirituality wrapped around me, the song of the mountains and the yak and the quiet gentle folk in the fields. I would hate to see that swept away by the 'superior' wisdom of the West.

It could also simply be an association with sickness and Pheriche for me. David junior, our student cameraman from Ballyfermot College of Further Education, had need for the hospital services and was diagnosed with tonsillitis. He struggled on for another day or two, but it was really the death knell for his expedition and shortly Pat would turn him around. I also got agonisingly sick myself in Pheriche. It was nothing to do with the pizza surprise for David senior, David Walshe from Cork, who was celebrating his birthday in style. After a week of eating pasta, rice and potato stew, with fried eggs and chips with everything, pizza was amazing. I enjoyed dinner and think we even managed to rustle up a bottle of wine, but when I went to bed the sickness struck. I knew what it was instantly and it had nothing to do with altitude. I had total certainty of that. I had felt bloated for the previous three days and sensed there was a build-up of fat occurring in my body. I have no gall bladder and the consultant had warned me that without the gland to regulate the flow of bile, I couldn't entertain a high-fat diet for long. I had been dieting for so long before, during and after the operation that I had forgotten what would happen if my fat stores built up. The diet we were eating was necessarily heavy in fats because of the huge number of calories that we burn at altitude. Certain foods were difficult to transport by yak, and ironically, although we were headed for an icy landscape we needed to go through extremes of heat to get there and had no way of refrigerating fresh meat. So our diet consisted of high-energy carbs and fats, which would travel relatively lightly but add many calories to a meal. Fried eggs, fried potatoes, butter and full-fat yak milk. I was paying the price: my gut wrenched with pain and my back arched in agony as I tried to get through the night. There was nothing I could do except stay close to the bathroom and ride it out until my body cleared itself. I was calm by morning, but physically exhausted and mentally drained; and today we needed to walk again . . .

Day 7—Teena's blog—Pheriche

I found the warrior within. Today was a day for acclimatising, pushing up to 16,000 ft behind Pheriche for tea, before returning back to base for a second night. I thought it would be easy, that this was a 'rest' day because we weren't moving on to a new destination. Wrong! It was a brutal, long, hard haul. It should have taken two hours to get to the teahouse, but we made it in three, which failed to impress our expedition leader, now sometimes affectionately known as 'Grand Master Falve' . . . The breakout for me was on the return; after falling behind, I suddenly kicked into another gear and ran nearly a thousand feet up two hills to catch up. It was pure fury that fired me up and it felt amazing to romp home. They have an expression here, a greeting that you make on the trek, Namaste—'I greet the God within'. I doubt if I host a God, but today I found my warrior . . .

I expected to feel rough today after the night spent hugging my knees in a lonely bunk in Pheriche—and I wasn't disappointed. When Pat Falvey has 'rest day' written in an itinerary I seriously warn you to smell a rat. I don't know what that man does to relax, but trekking up a terraced hill to 16,000 ft above the sea is not exactly my idea of kicking back! Jenny and I both gave the big man grief, perhaps not verbally, but there were waves of mutiny glowering out from venomous, heavily lashed eyes, the sort of behaviour that our leader seems to find highly entertaining. Jenny pushed ahead with Rob and George. Phil was up above with Pat and his team. Rosaleen and Viv and the two Daves were somewhere behind me, while Ed was slightly ahead with his mate Hugh Chaloner, our professional and hugely talented photographer, who would later stun us all with the beauty with which he had captured our adventure. I was stuck in my usual spot, on my own about two-thirds down the line on a highway to nowhere, knowing we would make 16,000 ft and then head back down another couple of thousand feet to overnight again in Pheriche. It was hot and dusty, the farms all around smelt strongly of goat and what goats do . . . and I was cranky. I even think it rained, or maybe that was delusions kicking in and merging with cold, wet and windy days back on Carrauntoohil. Anyway, I was thick as two planks—arriving into a hut for tea after three hours to hear Pat commenting on how we were behind time by almost an hour. Looking back, I was clearly exhausted from the night before, but I didn't really see that then. I was always carrying the fear that my strength might go and each time I felt under pressure I tried to fight it.

The fight kicked in on the way back down to Pheriche. I was never a runner. I'm running now, but I didn't run then, and occasionally jogging down Spink was about the most I'd ever done that was faster than a brisk walk. Today I was striding out and walking as fast as I could and I still couldn't catch the leaders. Suddenly I started to run. I didn't plan to and I certainly didn't have a discussion with myself about it. I just started to run, with sheer bad-tempered fury and rage at the damned inadequacy of my stupid short legs. I ran and then I ran faster—possibly not the best tactic for acclimatising when everything is about moving slowly and not upsetting the body's equilibrium, but I was beyond logic, I was furious. I caught up with Ed and he looked at me in astonishment. You have to grin when you lock eyes with Ed. I loved this team that was travelling through this amazing country with me. We girls were Trojans, Amazonians who so knew we weren't and we cracked ourselves up laughing at our plight and the state of our hair and nails and the deep tan we all sported, which looked suspiciously like dirt. But Ed and Pat's guides, Tony and Mark, were my guardians. Tony's humorous reassurances got me through the first week when my confidence was shaky, Mark took me under his wing towards the end, but 'Dr' Ed mothered us all; Pat, guides, Sherpas, natives and even the yaks if they'd let him close enough. Advice was always on hand for any problem or condition. Dr Ed was always ready with a bag of tricks that had everything from blister pads to homeopathic remedies to chocolate— so much chocolate. Running towards Ed now, his big crinkly eyes broke into a grin when he saw the expression on my face and his dark corkscrew curls danced around his newly grown pirate beard as he started to run too. 'Let's go get 'em, girl,' he laughed; and we did!

Day 8—Teena's blog—Labouche / Gorak Shep

Our 'rest day' in Pheriche started with an acclimatising walk which took up five hours in the morning—and continued with a couple of hours of fixed rope work in full gear, with ice-picks and crampons on the hills behind us, as night began to fall. Practising the arrest techniques we'll need to stop us falling at full speed off an ice wall, I smacked my face off a rock. My teeth are still intact, but packing at 6 a.m. to trek uphill to Labouche, I was happy to leave our 'rest day' behind! Labouche brought its own surprises—no Internet, no phone signal and the now familiar stench from the 'drop loos' masked only by suffocating kerosene fumes that forced tears from our eyes. Vivian, my 'roomy' and I fell back on copious quantities of our one luxury, a tub of Chanel No. 5 that I'd bought in duty free on the way out. The combined essence was probably even more toxic, but we slept blissfully in denial, even if early morning brought puffy eyes and wheezing chests . . . Day 9 and Everest Base Camp beckons . . .

Labouche was heaving—in more ways than one. It was packed full of trekkers and the teahouse where we stayed was challenging for anyone with a sense of smell. More than a week in, myself and roommate Vivian reckoned we were seasoned travellers untouched by the hazards of smelly socks and drop toilets, but even we baulked here. Perhaps we were just having an off day. It really wasn't that bad, though; we were giddy as fools and probably quite irritating as we whispered and giggled our way through the night. If it wasn't for the freezing cold, and thin walls, and smelly toilets and lack of running water and bins of soiled toilet tissue, we could have been the boarding school twins from Malory Towers. Enid Blyton's schoolgirl series were my favourite books as a kid. I'd never had a sister and had dreamed of being a twin. Now this reminded me of those days. The bottle of Chanel No. 5 cream that I'd bought in duty-free in Dubai was one of the best expedition purchases I'd ever made, so take that, Mr Falvey! We girls shared it out between us each morning and evening, rubbing our arms and chapped faces and smelling the pretty, feminine scent. It was a true vanity and it made life bearable in the toughest conditions. Even the boys appreciated the effort, with bear hugs from Philip one morning as he exclaimed, 'Oh my God, you smell like girls!' . . . The simplest things were wonderful. Poor Jenny's braids had survived a week before driving her insane, and brushing out her hair was therapeutic for both of us. We had soft luminous eyes as we smiled at each other, friends forever. There were lifetime bonds made on this trip, the sort that are sometimes forged through sharing times of extreme physical effort and stress. We were all pushing ourselves beyond what we believed were the boundaries of our endurance, and small kindnesses took on momentous meaning.

It was really cold now, particularly at night. During the day I still walked in a vest. I walk hot and while I'm moving I just can't stand layering up, something I had no way of knowing until I got out here. But at night, when we ate and fell into our sleeping bags, the cold was biting and the walls of the teahouse so thin that my water bottle froze beside me. It seemed incredible to think that if we kept going with our challenge, we would soon be sleeping on ice, in tents. We were so close to Base Camp now that I could almost reach out and touch it. We'd lost some of the team: young David's tonsillitis has scuppered his chances—at least for now, and in floods of tears we left Rosaleen from The Hope Foundation behind to look after him at Pheriche. On the last walk out, Rosaleen walked with us for miles, before turning around and making her way back down to camp. That's true guts, turning around to help a colleague. I seriously didn't know if I had it in me to do that, after all those months of preparation. We all felt a huge loss for both David and Rosaleen. But they were to bounce back later . . .

Day 9—Teena's blog—Base Camp: 9 October

I've made it, I've done it. I've climbed to Base Camp Mount Everest; a gruelling, emotional odyssey that has transported me from 23 stone to the 'me' of the moment who has achieved the impossible. Ten months ago I promised to do this, but I never really thought I could, although I never really admitted I couldn't. I've lost 11 stone to get here and I'm 44 years of age. If I can do this, you can do anything. Today I commented to a colleague on reaching Base Camp that we had reached a platform of dreams. Dreams for those that climb higher than Everest and dreams for those that go back down to lives touched with the knowledge that the impossible is possible. My next challenge is Kala Patthar Mountain at 5 a.m., in preparation for making the summit of Island Peak. I'm not sure I can make it, but I'll give it a go. Whatever the result tomorrow, I'm bringing my dreams home . . .

I can't explain the feelings that charged through me as I walked into Base Camp with the Khumbu Glacier and icefalls wrapped around the trail, the majestic white-tops arched across a brilliant blue sky and the prayer flags lightly stirring in the cold breeze. It was a crystalline land surrounded by brightness and light. Many people say they're disappointed on walking into Base Camp because it's stony, lunar and barren. I thought it was the most amazing place in the world. I still might be imagining it, but I truly believe I was the first in. That doesn't make sense and it may not be right, but I can't ask my colleagues for fear they shatter my illusions! So, let me keep this one between you and me. Vivian joined me and we hugged and gasped, and spoke silent words about the months of training and planning that had brought us to this point and the lasting friendship that we knew without saying would stretch long into the future, even as the present became the past. We turned around and saw David senior had stopped just short; after giving everything he had, his feet had seized just short of his goal. As one we swept down on him—the poor man was probably only pausing for breath but we swept him up on female wings and half carried him across the portal, laughing and gasping at his protestations. There were tears for all three of us. What a moment, what an achievement, what a memory.

We knew that going home it really didn't matter at that moment what life might throw at us; we had this. It was clear for all to see that after this trip Jenny and Rob would also have each other. George, Ed, Philip, Tony, Pat, Mark, Hugh, the Daves, the girls, our new couple and the Sherpas . . . Nobody comes to this spot without a story to tell, a life-force and ambition, a need to prove something to oneself and to one's spirit. Whatever our motivation, we had all climbed our own mountains and we had all proved to ourselves that the impossible is possible. To prove a point, as we made our way down, we met Rosaleen and David junior on their way up. They had regrouped, refocused and returned, trekking the whole way up to

Labouche with a solitary Sherpa who'd stayed behind with them. They were now on their way to Base Camp and it was clear they were travelling well and going to make it. I told you that lady had guts.

What my colleagues didn't notice as we stood looking around before heading back down was the stony pyre that I built among the prayer flags. It joined countless others built by locals to mourn those who have died on the mountain. My marker was remembering my mum. I always knew there would be a reckoning and I think I always knew it would be here. In this frozen lunar land, I finally opened a box in my mind and released the feelings I'd locked on ice for over seven months. Quiet tears of release mixed with tears of joy before I rejoined the group to head slowly back down to Gorak Shep.

Chapter 10
Beyond Everest

Day 10—Pat's blog—Base Camp and Kala Patthar: 10 October 2010

Pat rang to report the teams' success in reaching Base Camp and climbing to summit of Kala Patthar (meaning 'black rock' in Nepali). Kala Patthar appears as a big brown bump below the impressive south face of Pumori (23,494 ft). At the wind-swept summit ridge, after a five to ten minute scramble over boulders, the top is marked with prayer flags and the views from here of Everest, Lhotse and Nuptse are spectacular. With emotion in his voice, Pat spoke of the journey so far, the team's determination and positive attitudes to challenges they have had to face. The weather has changed becoming overcast and Pat talks of the cold air surrounding him as he calls—standing outside the teahouse, the teams' home for another night before they leave in the morning for Island Peak Base Camp. Pat has turned three of the team around today—a decision made in consultation with the team. While Vivian, David F. and David W. now commence descent, their contribution to the team and their own personal success is a credit to them and the attributes they have given to the team will be carried forward in the team's attempt on Island Peak.

Day 10—Teena's blog—Beyond Everest Base Camp

Today we climbed Kala Patthar mountain at 18,209 ft, the same height as high base camp for Island Peak. The climb is part of our acclimatisation, but it's also a challenge in its own right. We left at 4.30 a.m. to catch the sunrise on the way up. It was bitterly cold and this was also something we needed to experience in preparation for our final challenge. Off we set across a sandflat, double-gloved, in thermals and balaclavas, and within minutes my drinking water had frozen in its insulated Platypus or carry-pouch. The drag up was excruciating. I was overheating with exertion although my fingers were stinging with the cold, and altitude was robbing me of oxygen, making every breath a gasp for air. I kept moving onwards and upwards, remembering the life-mantra I'd been preaching for the past 10 months of training 'one foot in front of the other'. Finally the sun burst over the surrounding snowy peaks and hit the team as it struggled upwards. Gloves and down jackets abandoned we made it to the top, after two and a half hours of climbing. We exchanged greetings with several other climbers arriving from around the globe, took pictures and picnicked on Snickers. In the middle of the celebrations my eye took me further, to a stony spur jutting up from the summit. To my surprise I found myself edging up there, ignoring the plummeting drop on either side. Well, I'd come so far . . . it seemed a waste not to. Don't know what happened to my dread of heights, maybe it's the altitude. Happy in my world above the world, I noticed one of our Sherpas had spotted me and captured my moment on camera. I've got to get that snap.

Kala Patthar didn't take that long, but it was a struggle and a clear indicator of tougher times ahead. At just over 18,000 ft it was knocking us for six; the air was thin and each step a struggle. We left Gorak Shep in the dark with our head torches lighting the way as we climbed down into an ancient lake bed, before climbing again and beginning the main ascent, which was steep and unforgiving. It was a trek, but a difficult one, made more uncomfortable by the bitter cold. My insulated Platypus froze in minutes, and left me carrying a 2-litre block on my back. It also left me short of fluids and as the climb continued I got very hot. It wasn't ideal, but I had to put up with it. Kala Patthar's name means 'small brown mountain' and that's what it is, with very little appeal in itself. Its true value would be revealed at dawn and Pat was pushing us hard, because he knew where he wanted us when the morning splashed over the top of the world.

I said earlier that Vivian might surprise us all with her grit and determination and this mountain was her triumph. She was never meant to trek any further than Base Camp, but when we set off this morning, she tentatively shrugged on her down jacket, double-gloved and with a grim look set off to face the night with the rest of the team. Pat called her up top, the spot she always dreaded from those days back on Carrauntoohil when the call would rattle out around the hills: 'Vivian' . . . She hated being the focus of attention, but Pat's guiding rules put the slowest climber first to set the pace and set the pace she did. It was a tough climb and Vivian probably found it toughest, but she pushed and pushed and never gave in, although you could see she was hurting.

The cold was astounding, a bitter wind whipped through us, increasing the wind-chill factor, and our faces burned with the biting savagery of the night air as we fought for each ragged breath. As we climbed the air grew thinner but the light grew brighter and suddenly we could sense the dawn approaching as we closed in on the top of the summit. Our steps grew lighter and our smiles wider as the approach of the sun brought vitality and strength back to the group— amazing the effect it had, it was a hugely powerful moment. I think Pat must be an old master at timing sunrise on a mountain; he pulled the same spectacular on Purple Mountain many months ago back in Kerry. In this case we were about to realise Kallapattah's true specialty. Suddenly the new day burst forth over Everest herself, Chomolungma, Sagarmatha, Mother Goddess of the Earth, illuminated and finally on view in her entirety, displayed to us from our perch high on the top of this small brown mountain. We had seen partial views and glimpses of the Goddess for days now, but this was the first time that we could clearly see the magnitude of the distant mountain from base to peak. The view was spectacular and prompted terror and awe in all of us as we watched the mountain unfolding. We warmed quickly with the sun and I've never been happier for anyone than I was for Viv at that moment. Shortly afterwards we headed back down, aware that Vivian would join the two Davids in turning down the mountain, but while I'd lost my roomie, I knew she was happy to go and thrilled with what she'd achieved, which was far more than she or we had expected or imagined. Another impossible dream realised and exceeded.

Day 11—Teena's blog—to Island Peak

We've made Everest Base Camp and climbed Kala Patthar and now the final and biggest test is looming. Today I got my first real sight of Island Peak. Jesus. Realisation hit for the first time of what I'm crazy enough to be considering. Christ. It's a bloody mountain. I mean a craggy, icy, jagged, real life mountain, at 20,300 ft—higher than Everest Base Camp and a technical climb needing harness and crampons and ice axes. What am I doing? Who am I kidding? I stared in disbelief at the summit and ridge off in the distance, as the team traversed the changing countryside, leaving flora behind and headed for tundra as we made our final approach. With the challenge to Island Peak looming, Team Hope gathered in the evening for a technical briefing from expedition leader Pat Falvey. Our challenge was now switching from trekking to technical. Looking around I could see for the first time that my fellow colleagues were also feeling doubtful and tired. We have reached two of our three key objectives and are now wondering about moving to the next level. A haunting, moving, soul-searching day . . .

I was terrified. I walked along the tundra looking into the distance and the icy towers that were moving towards us and it was all I could do to breathe with the adrenaline surging through my veins. I looked around the team. Jenny's knee still hurt. Rob was suffering brutally from altitude; he'd lost a lot of weight, felt sick most of the time and was getting headaches. He hadn't developed AMS, but he wasn't in great shape. He and Jenny had acknowledged what we had seen for days and they now walked together comfortably, sometimes holding hands. It was sweet and we were all happy for them; they are both lovely people and seemed ideally suited. 'Dr Ed' was tired and looked stressed but seemed strong otherwise; his mate Hugh Chaloner, our photographer, was suffering headaches. Philip was charging along like a tank but looked like he'd done eight rounds with Mike Tyson: his face was swollen and he looked bruised around the mouth and nose. Rosaleen was suffering too—she'd developed agonising acid reflux and her nose was badly burned by the sun and frost and looked very sore. Tony Nation, Pat's guide who had got me through the first tough hike to Namche, also had problems; his lip had split quite badly and he was clearly in quite a lot of pain. Mark Orr, his colleague, was unfazed and had replaced Tony at my side and Pat just plodded as he always did, seemingly inexhaustible—never elegant, but never stopping, just powering through quietly and without fuss like a slow, deep wave.

Physically I was in surprisingly good shape. I felt little or no ill effects from altitude, no headaches, no nausea, no dizziness, my legs and knees were sound, I hadn't lost weight, I was drinking 4 litres of water a day and was well-hydrated, my ankle was pretty much recovered. Mentally it was a different story; my heart was racing and my imagination running into overdrive as I thought of the glacier and the crevasse ahead that we'd have to cross, of the icewall and then the snowy ridge-walk to the summit. I did a radio link back to 98FM sounding upbeat, positive and enthusiastic, but afterwards when the tape stopped rolling I admitted to my news anchor, Orlaith Farrell, that things weren't going well. 'I'm really doubting myself,' I confessed. 'I really don't think I can do this.' 'Aw, Teena, I'm sorry,' came Orlaith's soft Irish tones, like a hug all the way from Dublin. I wrapped it around me and said good night, promising both of us that I'd do my best. Speaking with Orlaith reminded me of home, of the news team that had pulled together to support me while I juggled work and training and fundraising—and before that, when I was sick. 98FM is a great radio station to listen to and it's probably clear that we all get on from the cheekiness that works its way out onto the airwaves, but I can't talk about the year that got me to this point if I don't send a hug back to Dublin for the talent and strength that backed me when I needed it and had the faith to let me go ahead and jump off Ferris wheels and climb glaciers. One of the crew told me afterwards that they really thought I'd kill myself—

I'm so glad they didn't tell me at the time! With my main challenge completed and the seductive menace of Island Peak now hurtling towards me, I also thought of the listeners who were following my blog and the spot satellite tracker on the website back at home, and the supporters who had helped me lose weight and raise money for Hope. What were they thinking? Were they expecting me to go for the big one? Should I even be considering that? This had to be my decision. I worried about Dad and hoped he wasn't worried about me. I'd asked before I came out if he was scared for me. Usually a man of few words and not normally given to 'flowery stuff' as some would put it, he surprised me with his answer. He looked me straight in the face and said, 'You were dying. Your mother and I were prepared to bury you before us. Why would I be worried at what you're doing now? Better to die living than to live dying.'

No one on the team was talking much on this stretch and as usual I was walking on my own, thinking my own thoughts and sinking my own ship. I didn't let on how I was feeling, which was probably a mistake because I was brewing myself a whole pot of trouble. The final walk into Base Camp for Island Peak was for me the hardest day so far. It was back to my speed again. I couldn't keep up with the lead group and it was almost more exasperating because this particular stretch was relatively flat, along an ancient frozen river delta. I felt I should be able to keep up, but no matter how hard I pushed, the team were still out in front. At the end of the day I finally made it into Base Camp for Island Peak, exhausted and mentally in trouble. Pat seemed to emerge from nowhere. 'Are you alright, girl?' he asked. I sobbed, 'I'm too slow, I'm too slow,' beside myself with disappointment and choking back bitter tears. Pat gave me a big bear hug and reassured me that I wasn't too slow, that I had just made the time. I hadn't realised he must have been timing us; it never occurred to me that he was watching everything and all of us, always. It hadn't really struck me how great his personal responsibility for us all was. In hindsight, leading a mixed group of amateurs through hazardous terrain must be daunting. I took his reassurance now, but I still felt rattled—because being fast enough or not, I still hadn't been able to catch the leaders and how would that translate on the glacier?

Day 12—Pat's blog—Island Peak Base Camp: 12 October

It's Tuesday . . . it's after 7.30 p.m. (2.52 p.m. Irish time). We are all at Island Peak Base Camp moving to High Camp tomorrow . . . making attempt the following morning in the early hours. All the team are in good form.

Day 12—Teena's blog—Island Peak Base Camp

I'm out! Today we trekked our way to Island Peak Base Camp . . . and I bailed. The hike was tough but I walked well into Base Camp, the tents were set, we drank soup in the mess and I was game for the challenge ahead. Shortly afterwards Team Hope headed for an acclimatisation walk to Island Peak High Camp. We walked along a gully and turned towards the mountain to begin to climb. I stared up at the dark, grainy boulders reaching into the sky, and strained my neck to search for the outline of the summit against the cold, blue, bright evening sky. Catching the eye of expedition leader Pat Falvey, I slowly drew my finger across my throat, turned on my heel and headed back down the mountain . . . alone.

I don't think anyone saw it coming—least of all me. Just after settling into Island Peak Base Camp we headed up the valley for an acclimatisation walk towards Island Peak High Camp. We were now so close to the glacier that I could see its frozen reaches, from the bottom of the rocky gully we were about to scramble up. The rocks were black and oppressive and the dark mass of it seemed to press in around me. It wasn't a difficult scramble, but my mind was far beyond the dark rocks. I was off on a flight of fancy, on the glacier above and beyond that to the headwall.

I toyed with it in my mind, chewed on what lay ahead and asked myself how I would feel if I quit now before I got into difficulty on the glacier and screwed up the entire expedition. I decided that I wouldn't feel bad at all: I rationalised that this last challenge was simply beyond my capabilities. I hadn't expected it would be this way. I was in the wrong gig on the wrong day; I was ordinary, a 44-year-old journalist struggling with her weight and totally out of her depth on a mountain in Nepal. My own negative thoughts finally subsumed me and I made my dramatic departure from the group, grabbing the boss's eye and drawing a finger across my throat from ear to ear, before I slipped away and started the lonely walk back down to Base Camp.

The Sherpas were great; no flashes from surprised eyes, just a gentle welcome back to the mess tent, a chair pulled out and a gentle inquiry if I would take soup. I thanked the mess team and gratefully drank the hot noodle broth and waited for the others to arrive. When the team finally did return, they were all clearly exhausted, but they gathered around me with hugs, all wishing me well, giving me pep talks and suggesting I'd have another go tomorrow. I calmly told them my mind was made up, I wasn't begging for plaudits or flattery or persuasion, I knew when I was done, I told them. We hugged nonetheless and then ate dinner in the mess tent.

We had switched to tents shortly after leaving Everest Base Camp and never had I experienced such cold as lying on ice with just a thin membrane between me and the outer world. Despite the discomfort, to my surprise I loved the tents, the simplicity of staying in them, the freedom of movement, the fact that there were no bad smells or trapped cooking fumes like there were in the huts. There was no denying it was hard. I would lie laced into my sleeping back with every conceivable flap closed against the cold and still just a small move like turning a leg or a foot would send a cold shaft of air piercing its way down between my shoulder blades. There are various theories among mountaineers about the benefit of sleeping in bags with or without clothes. Some argue that clothes reduce the effectiveness of the bag's ability to trap body heat, others argue that's rubbish. I tried both systems and was equally cold regardless!

Drinking volumes of water to stay hydrated usually means getting up in the middle of the night to answer calls of nature. The torture of unfurling from the relative warmth of the sleeping bag to hit a wall of freezing air made me resist those urges as long as possible and inevitably I'd find myself gasping to dash for the door of the tent, but I couldn't bear the cold without dressing and couldn't step outside without boots, so by the time I reached relief, I was gasping to pull the thin air into my lungs, my chest heaving with exertion and the effects of altitude as I struggled back in to undress and try and get some warmth again, totally exhausted. The cold nights were not pleasant and no human should see their own pee freeze as it hits the deck!

We were staying two in a tent and I was now sharing with Rosaleen. The large mess tent was for socialising and eating. We went back there now after dinner to discuss our plans for the next day. Pat was briefing the team and explaining that tomorrow we would break camp and move again to High Camp, setting up again in the new location at close to 18,500 ft, before pushing off the following morning for the final stretch. We would practise fixed rope techniques for Island Peak before we broke camp and before making the final attempt on the summit. He made no mention of my exit from the group, no attempt to persuade me to stay, then finally at the end of the briefing he looked across and asked what I would be doing. I thought for a moment and said I'd scramble up to High Camp with the rest of the team and practise the fixed rope technique, but I wouldn't be joining them on the glacier. Briefing over, we had final cups of coffee and tea, and headed off to our icy beds.

Day 13—Teena's blog—High Camp Island Peak

I'm back. Today Team Hope practised fixed rope technique at Island Peak Base Camp and then trekked up to High Camp; a tough 2.5 hour hike across steep and rough terrain. When we reached High Camp, we broke for soup and then began an acclimatisation hike up towards the ridge that would begin the technical climb for Island Peak. An hour into the climb and about a third of the way up, the team called halt and prepared to turn around and go back down to make camp for the night. Before we moved off, we had an impromptu briefing on the cliffside as expedition boss Pat Falvey asked us whether we were capable of making it to the top of the ridge tomorrow. He stressed that we'd need the strength to accomplish that and THEN climb a mountain, and pointed out that any late turn-arounds would rob the team of Sherpas and guides and add to the risk. From somewhere within I felt a quiet confidence descend and heard myself saying with certainty that I could do it. Folks, I'm back . . .

The madness of the past 24 hours passed away quietly that day. Somewhere on a rock above Island Peak High Camp and when I least expected it, I got my mojo back! I didn't expect to put myself back onto the team for Island Peak—just a short time earlier I had completely talked myself out of it. But as we ran through the last checks just hours before the final push, I knew with quiet confidence and certainty that I could do it. I don't know where the calmness came from, in the same way that I had no idea where the terrors of the past few hours had materialised from. Part of my anxiety had been a fear that I would slow down the team on the glacier and ruin it for everyone, because once we passed onto the ice, turning someone around and back down the mountain would be impossible without losing one of the treasured Sherpas. Whatever shift had happened in my mental state, I was now determined that this wouldn't happen; I wouldn't be a loose link any more. I knew I had proved my mettle already on this trip and I finally accepted what Pat had said days ago, when he said I wasn't the fastest but I was quick enough to make it. I was confident about my rope skills after all the hours training back on the Trinity College climbing wall. I was confident that I could tie on in the dark, after practising knots at home in my bedroom with the lights out. Hours of snapping on crampons made me confident I could boot up quickly and efficiently at the top of the gully ahead and after hours of running up the steps at Spink, leg-pressing 110 kg in the gym, banning the use of the lift at work and walking all eight flights of stairs every day, I knew this would all stand to me now on the headwall when we needed to kick in with our crampons and move slowly up that mountain of ice. All these positive images and messages were flooding my mind and forcing away the terrors. I wasn't cocky, I knew it might still prove too much for me, but I was sure I had earned a chance to try and I wasn't giving that up without a fight. I didn't realise any of this until I heard that final prompt from Pat to the group: 'Who's in?' It was as if

I was watching from a distance as I heard myself answering, 'I'm back.'

Day 13—Pat's blog—Island Peak High Camp: 13 October (2 p.m. Irish time)

Weather is good and holding, first summit attempt by all Island Peak team members in six hours approx. Everybody is a little tired but all looking forward to the climb.

We pushed off in the middle of the night for the gully. It was bitterly cold, but none of us felt it. We were sombre and excited in equal measure. Everything had led to this crucial moment and it was all there for the taking. Pat turned Rosaleen before we left. It was heartbreaking and she was devastated, but it was the leader's call and he believed she just didn't have the speed. I scraped in and replaced Vivian at the front of the group—the slowest climber leading under Pat's rules. The irony after such a long journey and such an epic trial to get here; and now through no glorious cause but due to borderline ability, I was actually leading Team Hope up the final stretch. We set off, head torches shining sharply into the cold, bright night. I picked my pace and off we went. It was nerve-wracking leading from the front and I understood how Vivian had felt. I started to worry if I was going too slowly for the group. If we were too late getting to the glacier the sun could come up and start melting the ice, making it more dangerous to cross. Or perhaps I was allowing the moment to get to me and I was moving too quickly and was about to scupper my chances by burning out too early. Very quickly I had a conversation with myself based around the need to get a grip and stop wasting energy with more fanciful thoughts. My Tipperary mountain man came back, telling me to climb my own mountain, and that's what I focused on. I picked my pace, as I had done every day for the past two weeks, walking on my own as I had done when I was trotting along two-thirds of the way back down the line. Step by step, one foot in front of the other, and forward we went.

After a while we noticed a line of lights dotted out below us and realised there was another group climbing from below. We figured out that it was a group of advanced Italian climbers who we had met briefly at Base Camp the day before. They were skipping High Camp and taking on Island Peak directly from Base Camp, adding several extra hours and nearly 2,000 ft to their journey but sparing the expense of setting up a second camp. They moved like a machine and we all felt the pressure of them moving up behind us. They looked like soldier ants coming at us from far below and I imagined I could feel the mountain vibrate beneath their boots as they approached closer to our mark. Total fantasy, of course, but we all felt the oppression of being eaten up by a group of clearly superior physical strength. I think that perhaps the competitive streak in Pat gave a jolt and he hovered close to suggest I picked up the pace. I considered it and felt deeply moved to pick up, but after a moment replied with total conviction that we could all brace ourselves for being overtaken, because this was my pace. They passed us, and the mountain didn't shake, vibrate, landslide or avalanche. We survived and kept moving upwards. It was a long, exhausting climb and scramble which lasted for about 2.5 hours.

Finally we made the glacier, snapped on our crampons and the real journey began. Dawn broke as we set off across the frozen ice. I've said it before, but Pat's timings are truly impeccable when it comes to sunrise and sunset on a mountain. God, it was beautiful. The white ice and snow swept around us in waves like sand-dunes in the Sahara, gently undulating, rising and falling away from the gully towards the beautiful peaks in the distance and the rectangular, jagged form that is Island Peak. She was entrancing, seductive as we moved across the ice. We were roped together as we had practised on the MacGillicuddy Reeks, in case one of us slipped into a crevasse. A glacier is a moving entity, always shifting and changing, and fissures and cracks develop with time and are not always apparent if covered in a shallow bridge of snow or ice. We moved as close as we dared to one deep crevasse which we traced all the way to Island Peak. The colour of the landscape was extraordinary with the pink wash of early morning light touched from blush to gold as the sun moved higher, and the ice turning from white to blue as it dropped off towards the crevasse. Blue ice is dangerous, the Sherpas warned us, as we moved away from the edge and started the traverse to the headwall that lay up ahead in the distance. There was a long, long way to go yet and all with crampons digging in to gain purchase on the ice. I'd never been in snow or ice before, not like this. I've never been on a skiing holiday; the most snow I've ever seen was a snowball fight back home at Christmas. Walking on this surface in this way was strange and new and very tiring on the legs. But we took it one step at a time. I was no longer in front, can't remember how or why that happened. Somehow when we roped up, I found myself back in my natural spot, two-thirds of the way back down the line!

Day 14—Pat's blog—Back at Island Peak Base Camp: 14 October 2010

We are all back at Island Peak Base Camp! Seven of the Hope Team and three Sherpas summitted. We have just had dinner. Everyone's in good form and tomorrow, we commence our descent to Kathmandu.

So here I am, hanging on the edge of an icy wall, at the very spot where you came in. Some of us make it up here and some of us don't. When we came to the foot of this headwall the amazing Sherpas moved ahead to set up a fixed rope and in my mind I was back on a dirty slab in the middle of a warm wet Kerry dream— remember? There was no particular order about who went first up the rope, but no one seemed to be moving. I tied on and started moving up the wall. I'm pretty sure George jumped on behind me and later I think he overtook me. I think that was the order, but there's a sense of unreality about the detail, perhaps caused by altitude and simple lack of sleep. I struck out and up and kicked with my feet into the ice. It was softer than I expected and my crampons slid down a few inches. I wasn't expecting that and it unsettled me. I kicked off again and got a little higher but the same thing happened and I slipped down the wall a little further. I went again. I clearly lacked technique here. I looked up above and saw that George seemed to be moving more smoothly than me. He had turned his crampons slightly sideways, while I was sure we needed to be toes in, but I was willing to change tack if that would help. Bit by bit I kicked and pushed my way up the wall, my ice axe in my left hand, pushing off the wall for balance and my right hand pushing up my jumar. Using a jumar helps, but your legs need to do most of the work because they're a bigger muscle group and arm muscles burn out too quickly.

Pat had warned us time and time again that we'd have to use our legs to get up that wall. It's a steep pull up around 330 ft and it's exhausting. I got to around 200 ft and stalled. I had pushed and pushed and pushed, but my legs were gone. The muscles were shaking and screaming and I just didn't have the strength. I jammed my frame against the ice and the rope and pushed back off to try and ease out my spine and my thighs, while I thought about what I could do next. I couldn't believe I had ground to a halt for lack of strength. My nightmare scenarios involved crampons falling off on the glacier, slipping over the edge of a crevasse and the rope breaking, slipping off the summit ridge and plunging thousands of feet to an icy grave . . . but not giving in to the bog-standard condition of simply being knackered. I was panting and probably panicking a bit, but my breathing wasn't actually that bad, my fitness was actually okay, it was simply my leg muscles that had burned out.

It felt like an eternity as I hung there on the rope figuring it out, but it was probably just a minute or two. I looked up and had absolutely no idea how I was going to get to the ridge above, and then I looked down to the rest of the team over 200 ft below and I knew with absolute certainty there was no way I was going back down. My eye caught sight of the ice axe in my left hand. The tall blunt end stuck in the ice like a walking stick, supporting my balance, and I looked fascinated at the business end, the long hook-like blade, which up to now had been redundant. I grasped the insulated shaft of the axe firmly in my hand, drew my arm back across my shoulder and let fly, swinging it across the ice, as far up as I could reach and as hard as it could hit. It caught and held and I pulled myself up with my left arm, pushed the jumar up with the right and pulled up again, then swung the axe with my left and went again. I heard Pat or someone shout, 'Legs, legs,' from far below; I ignored them. Actually I may have shouted something ungrateful back down the line. I may not have been following the rules, I may not have been doing it 'right', but I was doing it and I was moving again. I basically dragged myself up the last 100 ft with my arms and collapsed over the edge at the top, absolutely stunned that I had made it, hugging George on the top and laughing with the grinning Sherpas, who seemed really thrilled for me.

With my poor head for heights I'd been worrying about the next stage, the ridge walk to the summit, but after making it up that headwall, I felt that I skipped along the ridge without a care in the world. In reality, it was a slow, cautious slog, with just a narrow strip of snow-covered ice to climb along, with terrifying drops to either side. We all stepped slowly up the incline, breathing heavily and puffing between each breath, before finally making it to the top, to balance on the tiny 6-ft platform on the summit. In amazement I watched Philip paint his 'extreme art' pastel of the view from the summit. There was laughter and a buzz of conversation at the top, but chatty Teena for once fell silent. Nor could I sit down, but just kept gazing and staring all around me in all directions—thirstily gulping down this view, so special and so rare, and one which I was unlikely to ever see again. The skies had cleared to bright blue and the sun gleamed off the glacier, while a few flakes of snow fell around us.

Pat always said you hadn't climbed a mountain until you were sitting talking about it in a pub! It would take many days to get to a pub, but it was definitely time to move before we got cold and stiff. Jenny, Ed and I and Philip, George, Pat, Mark and the Sherpas all grinned widely at each other, knowing we had changed irrevocably in the last 24 hours and knowing instinctively that nothing would ever be quite the same. We had come 20,305 ft towards the top of the world and we knew without a shadow of a doubt that perseverance and faith could make the impossible possible. Bringing our dreams back down the mountain, we'd do our best to spread the word. You don't have to climb Everest, you don't have to climb a hill, but we all have our own mountains to climb in our hearts, and there's every chance of success if you hold firm, hold true, and concentrate on putting one foot in front of the other.

Day 14—Teena's Island Peak Report

I did it. Today I clawed and dragged my way to the summit of Island Peak. A technical climb for a greenhorn who'd only been trekking for the past six months and who'd never before had a set of crampons on her feet. Team Hope spent 10.5 hours on the mountain and not all of us made it. But I did, and I can't believe my body allowed me to do that. Hours of walking up a bouldered ridge, hours more dragging our way across a glacier, then the agonising climb up a sheer headwall of ice. Two-thirds of the way up, with my legs screaming, the harness cutting into my groin and my crampons refusing to get traction on the ice, I remember looking up to see how far I had to go. I knew at that moment with absolute certainty that I would get there, but with equal certainty I had no idea how! I remembered a comment from team leader Pat Falvey that getting to the top was 80 per cent in the mind. I dug in and lashed out with my ice axe and dragged myself up with my arms, slowly, screamingly, growling at myself and going again until finally I reached the top. Scaling my way up the final ridge walk and abseiling three ropes down a mountain seemed incidental after that. I was snowblind (temporary), the harness had cut my groin and my face was badly burned from the exposure and the sun at the height we'd reached. Sore, stunned and weary; but 'on top of the world' . . .